THE TESTIMONY

OF LOVE, STRUGGLES, FORGIVENESS, AND COMPASSION

EMELY DULIG DICOLEN, PhD

ISBN: 978-621-95272-1-7

DEDICATION

This book is dedicated to **ROD**
with whom the testimony evolved,
without whom, I could not have learned
genuine love, forgiveness, and compassion;

RENZ FRANCES
RACQUEL HELENA
REINIER JOSEF
ROCEV MIGUEL
My four living trophies,
without whom, I could not have learned true parenting with
God,
who made me holier and more faithful to God;

BROTHERS & BROTHERS-IN-LAW
(Constante, Rommel, Henrich, Martin, Dexter & Moises)

SISTERS & SISTERS-IN-LAW
(Merilyn, Rowena, Rizalyn, Ofelia, Rizza, & May)

NIECES & NEPHEWS
our true genuine family, without whom,
parenting and supporting my children
could have been impossible,
who loved me and my children unconditionally.

CONTENTS

COMMENTS

Blessed are you among women, Doc! Thanks for sharing this true to life story. It's really nice because it is topical. It's a good material for publication. I enjoyed reading your stories because they can be used in my homily. Thanks for sharing. I'm slowly becoming your avid fan. I'm deeply touched..."the Word alive!" - *Fr. Alfie, MSP*

The Testimony aims not to deny the necessity or promise of change but to underscore the extraordinary effort it requires: love, forgiveness and compassion to build a realistic foundation for achieving genuine progress in family relationships. - *Geralyn Panisales*

The story of this family is a testimony that the love and mercy of God is experienced even in the most painful moments of life. We just have to let God take control of the situation. I learned from this book that humility and strong faith in God can really free us from the chain of anger and bitterness. - *Clang Padoyao Eddio*

Many people are so imprisoned in their minds that the beauty of life does not really exist for them. This book and the author showed vividly life's 'rainbow colors.' This seems to be the 'right book' for many people at this point in time. I heartily recommend this profoundly inspiring book that promises love and forgiveness beyond all hurts and pains. Grab a copy! - *Ruth Layug Suba*

Great book! Your story has taught me to look at the challenges in life from another perspective. Very inspiring indeed! – *Maribel Rabang*

This book is interesting and inspiring. Most of all it encourages the readers to face challenges in life, not to depend on their own abilities and strength but rather depend on God's will because HE kows what is best for us. – ***Ruby Abagat Hargreaves***

After finishing Doc Ems' book, I know I had to share it. It's inspiring and practical. It shows a compassionate and forgiving heart while looking at the realities of the situation. At the end, she was saved by the legal document she has worked hard to get because she had the wisdom to pursue it. Her life story is one great lesson she is imparting to her children and to the wives and mothers around her. – ***Wendy Flor***

I am so thankful that I read The Testimony. I would say that you are a living testimony. God is very much glorified in your book. I am sure that many people will be blessed!! – ***Julita de Villa***

The Testimony unfolds a family's journey of love in the face of trials and struggles, and of mercy and forgiveness without boundaries; a life story that will inspire you to look at relationships with the eyes of God. - ***Mavic Tiongson Cortez***

I can't help but ask you this? Are you really a human being? I think you are an angel. God sent you to inspire thousands of people, whether you know them or not. I salute you, Ma'am!!! You deserve everything…" – ***Shaneil Dipasupil***

I am so happy that I can read a new book that you have written again!! :) Please continue making these kinds of books, because you are helping a lot of people. Please include me in your prayers. Take care and God bless! - Grace Laus
Thank you so much Ems for sharing your beautiful story. An INSPIRATION! You are so blessed. May God be with you

ALWAYS. – *Jeng Dizon*

So touching... I am a fan... Looking forward for more.- **Agnes Gabriel**

Doc Ems, you're so blessed. I was crying while reading your story…Forgiveness…heal the wounds in our heart. – **Charmee Magallanes**

I was really touched!!! The candid way you shared your story of forgiveness is very heart warming. Keep on!!! - **Veneranda Sajorda**

Speechless! Thank you, I suddenly took a deep breath and I asked myself? Have I totally forgiven my past, especially myself? - **Asiah**

Doc Emz...morning....I cried while reading it. Thanks for sharing us your true to life story. GOD BLESS! - Leah Espiritu I was deeply touched. God is good all the time. I'm so proud of your strength and you have such good children. God bless you more Ma'am Ems. – **Alice Cho**

Hayyy, teary eyed with your story Doc Ems. Congrats in advance for your upcoming book about your life. - **Cris Calaguas**

Thanks! Your post really blessed me. I do believe that prayer works and miracles will happen when we do believe it. God bless you. May I share this post in my wall? - **Felicia Shen**

I have read this article when you first posted it. I cried, really cried. I am reading it again, same amount of tears and emotion flow from within. In my mind I wished I had also the chance to see my father during his wake. Ems, I love reading your stories. God bless you my dearest friend! -**Precy Zablan**

Prayer works indeed! It's a very touching story. I cried while reading it. I can feel the pain of losing parents. God bless, Reinier. God bless you and your children. Love you Ate Ems.- ***Archana***

I look forward to your inspirations every day and I want to hug you tight. You are such an inspiration! – ***Marites Sado***

Ma'am Ems, good morning! How have you been? I read your piece on "Moving On" and I can't help but read all your write-ups. I wanted to thank you. Those writings touched me and gave me such inspiration and courage in these times of trials in my life. Thank you Ma'am Ems. God bless you po. – ***Marilyn Sumayo***

Ma'am Ems, I can relate with your story and I'm truly touched. I could feel your unwavering faith in God. How I wish I could do the same. Congratulations! In spite of the many trials and difficulties that came your way, you survived and you became more successful in your career. I am so proud that I met you and we became friends during my journey in Letran. I'm so proud of you. – ***Aida Elipse***

I just hope and pray that I could hug and kiss you like my Ina and say THANK YOU so much for touching my life. This book deepened my relationship with God, my family and other people. – ***Agnes Idos***

Thank you for sharing the grace of God. Thanks also to Him working in all that you've gone through. I found immense inspiration and hope and push and courage. It's a book that will definitely be on my top favorites. – ***Tina Rubio***

FOREWORD

The Author, **Dr. Emely Dicolen** has meticulously dissected God's Word, then like a music virtuoso she has meaningfully given its melody that harmonizes with one's own life. Inarguably, it is Doc Ems' (as she is fondly called) dedication to her vocation as Counselor and Educator, and her deep sense of faith in God that made this sequel of her first book "And God Smiled Back" possible.

In this book she wants to connect and reach out with people through sharing her life's story in order to make a difference in their lives and in their relationship with God. Undoubtedly, after climbing mountains and trekking rough roads of life, she opened the door for others to learn from the challenges that she has successfully hurdled.

Reading this collection of narratives, we can easily encounter how a doting mother, a faithful and committed wife, a "super woman" taught us practical theology of a person who believes that each and every one can better care and love others in the way God first loved us.

That LOVE simply means COMPASSION and FORGIVENESS.

To married couples who are earnestly trying to keep their relationship afloat and grow amidst changing situations and challenges, this book is an effective tool to understand one's imperfections and accept each other's human frailties. Thus, going through the pages of this diligent work of wisdom inspired by the Holy Spirit, the reader will be led to visit his/her own personal inner landscape. I should say the most provocative journey that is oftentimes ignored or taken for granted.

I highly endorse this book because it speaks not only to a specific group of people but to everyone from all walks of life. Perhaps, many would wonder and ask themselves, *"Is the author speaking directly to me?"* **Yes!** As Franz Kafka aptly puts it, *"many a book is like a key to unknown chambers within the castle of one's own self."*

Fr. Alfredo Africa, Jr., MSP
HFCC Chaplain

ACKNOWLEDGMENT

The Testimony of Love, Struggles, Forgiveness, and Compassion, is God's love made genuine and prosper in me through people who made another dream come to a reality. My gratitude and appreciation goes to…

- God, through the Holy Spirit, whose inspiration has given me the courage to be in touch with my inner self, the wisdom to write my experiences, and for sending people who have generously shared their time and resources to make this revelation;

- My children, Renz, Racquel, Reinier, and Rocev for unceasingly believing in me, for leading me to a life of devotion to God as well as fulfill my vocation both as a father and mother to them;

- My brothers, sisters, brothers-in-law, sisters-in-law, nieces, and nephews for patiently helping me in my parental duties to my children during my absence, and for continually supporting me morally and financially;

- My everdearest BFF Lilibeth Sale (and of course her hubby Dennis Sale), my prayer partner and generous benefactor, who have benevolently shared her resources to make the second printing of this book possible;

- My extended family in Korea: Cynthia, for constantly

reminding me that God loves me and that I and my children are chosen by God for a mission to make known the love and forgiveness of God to people. Thank you for allowing yourself to be God's instrument in encouraging me, with all humility and trust, to totally forgive Rod, myself, and my past; Mommy Ineng, for your motherly love and care. You have filled the longing for a mother in me, and for providing everything I needed especially during my busy days; Ardelle, for your constant reminder of "Ate, may awa ang Diyos," (God is merciful). These words have sustained me during those trying moments. Your obedience and unwavering faith in God is definitely admirable;

-	Friends whom I have always run to for moral support when I wanted to give up, and for financial help during those times when resources were scarce: Lilibeth, Marites, Flor, Matet, Precy, Lea, Norma, Ellen, Lyn, Edwin, Angeline, Carol, Elena, Alan, Juvie, Digoy, Rica, Ivy, Nomar, Tita Fe (for making a dream come true for my children to celebrate Christmas and New Year with me in Korea in 2010), Hermie and Kate, Joeffrey, Jhoanna, Joy, Fr. Alvin, Sr. Angel, Cynch (for adopting me and taking care of me after I was hospitalized due to acute gastritis), and Fr. Oh, Taek-Soo and his family (for teaching me Korean culture and considering me as part of their family during my three-month homestay)—you have definitely helped me and my children survive;

-	Letran friends who have journeyed with me during those fearful and anxious moments: Nina, for praying with me and keeping us safe and secure in your home; Au, for keeping me company during those nights that I dreaded going home; Jay, for listening to my stories and comforting me; Rica, for challenging me and helping us in our escape; Frs. Stephen and Audie for the trust and for finding ways to assist; Dean Bobi, Dean Almoro, Manong Boy, Bro. Boy, Sir Rufer, and Fr. Chris for risking their lives to help; Sharon and Ria for encouraging me when I was at my lowest;

-        Hyehwadong Filipino Catholic Community (HFCC) volunteers and church-goers, Fr. Glenn Jaron, MSP, Fr. Alvin Parantar, MSP, Fr. Alfie Africa, MSP, Fr. Arvin Mosqueda, MSP, Fr, Fredy, MSP, Fr. Percy Cinco, MSP, Mr. Stephano Yang, Mr. Han, Sheila, Marilyn, and Sr. Mikaela Santiago (for her prayers and for being my son's benefactress while he was in the minor seminary), who became my family when I came to Korea during the healing process. Your presence kept my sanity, your acceptance gave me the assurance that there is a family away from home;

-        All the Filipino communities and women migrant communities who have invited me to share my time and talent by giving recollections, values formation, trainings, and seminars, thank you for the confidence. In many ways you have inspired me to continue my apostolate;

-        Organizations who have trusted and believed in my capacity and who have allowed me to be of service to them: Association of Filipino Educators in Korea (AFEK or PhilRPG), Pinoy Iskolars sa Korea (PIKO), Filipino EPS Workers Association (FEWA), Association of Filipino Catholic Missionaries in Korea (AFCMK) and the Philippine Embassy in Seoul;

-        Korean colleagues from different universities who have supported me in many ways- Dr. Larry Chong and Dr. Sang-Ho Han of Gyeongju University; Dr. Ki-Joong Seong of Kyung-il University and his wife Esther, Dr. Kwang-Seok Lee of Kyungpook National University and Yeungnam University, Dr. Nam-Young Ok and Dr. Jeong-Woong Cheon of Catholic University of Daegu, and Dr. Sang-Yoon Ma of the Catholic University of Korea;

-        Rod, thank you for the love and the wonderful children you gave me. You have made me holier, indeed. And

to his immediate family- Daddy (RIP), Mommy, Roy (RIP),
and Ray, thank you for accepting me and my children as part
of your family. Marisa, thanks for remaining to be a good
friend and for helping Rod financially during his
hospitalization. To Rod's uncles, aunts, and cousins-thank you
that until the end your warmth, love, and acceptance remained.
Auntie Yda and Auntie Ruby, we have developed a very special
bond after Rod's death but it is never too late, thank you;

-         Prof. Assumpta Calano for voluntarily editing my draft
and the encouragement to share and write my story;

-         Mr. Stephano Yang who have willingly accepted the
laborious work of translating the book in Korean, and for
never saying no to whatever translation jobs I requested him;

-         To all the people who gave their comments, feedback,
and suggestions, especially Bro. Jimmy Villaflor to improve the
first draft of this book; and

-         YOU, who is, right at this moment, reading this book.
Thank you for allowing yourself to be touched, thank you for
allowing GOD to talk to you through *The Testimony*.

Emely Dulig Dicolen, Ph.D.

1 THE TESTIMONY

"Go home to your friends and tell them
how much the Lord has done for you,
and how he has had mercy on you."
Mark 5:19

IN MY INSPIRATIONAL BOOK, **AND GOD SMILED BACK**, I started with 1 Thessalonians 1:8. It says, "For from you the word of the Lord has sounded forth…in every place your faith in God has gone forth, so that we have no need to say anything "– YOU'RE the MESSAGE!

I commenced to write my reflections, insights and experiences and posted them on my Friendster account (Facebook, Twitter, Instagram, and other Social Networking Sites were still unheard of then). Most of them were published in the SAMBAYANAN Newsletter. Many of those who read my posts gave me positive feedback. They said they were touched, inspired, encouraged and moved by my sharing. Many of the readers were able to relate with the stories and personal experiences I shared on how GOD moved powerfully and mysteriously in these events in my life as a separated wife, a solo parent, a distant/cyber mom, an overseas worker, a missionary, a friend, a teacher… rolled into one – a servant of God.

These comments inspired me to compile all these reflections. With the help of close friends who edited and proofread the stories and generous patrons who financed the first publication here in Korea, the book was launched December 2008 at the St. Benedict Parish Church in Hyehwadong, Seoul, South Korea. Fr. Alvin Parantar, MSP, former Chaplain of the Hyehwadong Filipino Catholic Community (HFCC) and Fr. Andrew Kim, Rector of the Korean Missionary Society (KMS) (where I taught English to Korean seminarians before they were sent overseas), concelebrated the Eucharistic. The following are the links to the videos.

https://www.youtube.com/watch?v=LGYbWa4aHr0
https://www.youtube.com/watch?v=klUlSGq70T8

Prior to its launching, that was October 5, 2008, I sent an email to Fr. Domie Guzman, the Director of St. Paul's Publication inquiring about the possibility of publishing my book in the Philippines.   I received an answer the next day asking me to submit samples of my writings for evaluation.

On November 13, 2008, I received Fr. Domie's response and these were his exact words, "I FOUND THE SAMPLES INTERESTING FOR THEIR DIFFERENT TREATMENT OF THE WORD OF GOD… BASED ON THE LIVES OF FILIPINO MIGRANTS. PLEASE EMAIL THE WHOLE ELECTRONIC FILE OF THE MANUSCRIPT…..…"

St. Pauls finally published **And God Smiled Back** and launched together with other books on September 18, 2009 at the SMX Convention Center during the Manila International Book Fair.

The writer in me was born!

After that, people who have read the book have been asking me in person, through text messages and comments made on social network, *"Doc, kailan po yung susunod ninyong libro?"* **(Doc, when is your next book?)**. Since then, I planned writing the next one but it took years before it finally came to fruition.

THE TESTIMONY

My inspiration in writing my second book comes from my overwhelming experience of God who has kept His constant love revealed in the many challenges that I have gone through.

This desire of sharing how God manifested Himself in the midst of struggles in my life is overflowing especially these times when we are flooded with news of people both young and old who are experiencing different forms of depression, expressing behavioral problems, harboring thoughts on suicide or in the verge of committing murderous acts or other crimes. I also owe the writing of this book to everyone who remained steadfast waiting for this book. I am hoping and praying that this will give them the encouragement to see the world in a positive light in the context of faith.

This book is dedicated to all who:

- are going through depression;
- struggling parents/couples;
- couples with marital problems;
- children fraught with problems of absentee parent
- parents having problems with children;
- solo/separated/divorced/annulled parents;
- people who have difficulty forgiving others; and
- to anyone who wants to experience the love, forgiveness, mercy, and compassion of God in a very personal and concrete way.

On a very personal note, having decided to write and share about my/our struggles with my husband was not an easy decision to make because others, especially his family, might misinterpret it. While writing one of the chapters, God seemed to have asked me, *"Emely, are you ready to face and answer whoever questions you after these confessions?"* In my heart, I answered, *"Yes,*

Lord! I am ready!" I know God is completely in control, I have nothing to worry about because my intention is for His greater glory.

Besides, the mercy, compassion, and generosity of God shown in how we ended our story, is worth sharing. In prayer, I have asked Rod's consent, and in faith I believe he has given me permission to do so. I am sure that he was right beside me while writing, (today on the 9th month since he joined the Creator) because he also wants others to learn from us. Moreover, I know God wills this very wonderful story shared as a reminder of God's unfailing love. As he commanded, *"Go home to your friends and tell them how much the Lord has done for you, and how he has had mercy on you."*

LET US PRAY...

"Dear Lord, bless this person reading my testimony. Empower him/her with your Holy Spirit so that he/she may see you at work in the story. May he/she be inspired, touch his/her heart, speak to him/her, and let your constant and unconditional love felt right at this very moment. I ask this in the mighty name of Jesus. AMEN!"

POINTS TO PONDER...

1. Do you have any experience of God that is worth sharing? What is it?

2. Do you also feel the urge/inspiration to share your wonderful experiences with God to others? Why? How?

3. What possible obstacles have you encountered in testifying for God's love, mercy, and compassion? Why?

TALK TO GOD...

____
____
____
____
____
____
____
____

2 A TESTIMONY OF LOVE, STRUGGLES, FORGIVENESS, AND COMPASSION

So you should rather turn to forgive
and comfort him,
or he may be overwhelmed by excessive sorrow.
So I beg you to reaffirm your love for him.
For this is why I wrote, that I might test you
and know whether you are
obedient in everything.
2 Corinthians 2:7-9

THIS IS MY EULOGY during the wake of Rod. The first part is the English translation and the second part is the Tagalog version (verbatim). The videos are available on the following links:

https://www.youtube.com/watch?v=qp8XoGsKB7s
https://www.youtube.com/watch?v=I3CG4y5MELA
https://www.youtube.com/watch?v=o2NOSgYcS0E
https://www.youtube.com/watch?v=3Kv0esP4osg

ENGLISH

First of all I would like to say thank you. I am deeply happy that all of you who loved Rod, all of you who became part of Rod's story, and our story as a couple from the beginning, are here to witness the remaining hours that we have with him.

Last night, I gave a title to my testimony. Tonight, I will repeat my testimony not only because I'm not prepared or I have nothing to say but I will repeat my testimony because it is the summary of our story as husband and wife, our story as a family that I want to share with you. I hope that all of us will learn something from our history.

Our journey as husband and wife separated but reunited and became one family again. I said last night, that our story is a testimony of love, struggles, forgiveness, and compassion.

Why love? Why testimony of love? Rod and I began our relationship happy, sweet, caring… uncle, grandmother, auntie- -they all witnessed how we started. They saw us aspire to have a happy, wonderful family. It never came to us that our marriage will end this way. We never dreamt of being separated. All we wanted was to give our children the best future and have a simple life. Every moment in our more than three years of being boyfriend and girlfriend to ten or eleven years as husband and wife were full of love.

Yes! Struggles! These are inevitable in any relationship. As I said last night, my husband and I came from totally different family backgrounds. We have our own personalities, our own characters, and our strengths, and our own weaknesses which we tried to settle. We strived to settle our differences in a peaceful manner and even asked help when needed. We attempted to fight all these weaknesses and be together as a happy family. However, unexpected things happened. Those weaknesses gradually gave in to our inability to forgive, our incapacity to listen to each other that eventually led to the breakdown of the good marital relationship that we were guarding.

Yes, I admit in front of all of you here, I also have my weaknesses. Later on, I realized them one by one, too many to mention. But one of the weaknesses I discovered about myself was that I didn't know how to fight back, I didn't know how to shout, I didn't know how to ask for help even from my own family, thinking I could solve it myself. Rod has his own weaknesses too which I don't have to mention. Thinking that both of us can no longer mend those weaknesses, led us to our separation.

Our godmother told me a while back, it was so sad and disheartening that during those times when we were going through these struggles, no elder came to mediate. No elderly, who is more mature and who could understand the situation objectively intervened to make our relationship work. That is why we drifted apart… yes, we sadly drifted apart.

You know when "we," I say "we" because it was not just myself who decided to leave my husband. My children were with me in my decision. Rocev that time was still young. But I believed that they already had the capacity to decide, that is why it was our collective decision to leave.

So, why did I decide? I decided at that point when I was about to lose the self-respect I was holding on to, I was at the verge of losing the personhood I was clinging on to. And before I lose it, I deemed it necessary to leave. It was painful. It was a struggle. Maybe not all people will understand, but in my heart, and with my God, I knew He understood my decision.

Love. Struggles. Forgiveness. In those eleven years of separation, as what our godmother said, we knew in our hearts that my husband loved us so much. Every time my children and I were together, there was never a moment when we don't remember him. *What could have happened to your Papa? Is he ok? Is he well?* We love your Papa as I often told my children, *"do not blame your Papa. Your Papa loves you so much but he has some difficulty expressing his love."* That is why when we decided to meet him in March, the first time I hugged him again, I felt that love was still there. When my children hugged him as my facebook friends saw that on video, it was evident that forgiveness was sincerely felt in the heart of each one. On our way home, I asked my children how they felt. My eldest daughter answered, *"Mama, we felt like a thorn was removed from our heart."* How true it was!

That forgiveness gradually brought us back to constant communication by phone and text messaging with him because we knew that it is God's will that we will be all together again.

Then compassion, I shared this also with you last night. In the four or five days that we were together with the children, I've been constantly asking myself, *"Am I really kind? Am I a martyr? Or am I really forgiving by nature? Is God using me to accomplish a mission? To be a living witness to women like me? To people like me who have experienced or maybe experiencing what I have gone through?"* One time I told the children, *"you know, kids, I believe that we are chosen. Our family is chosen to testify about God's love, to testify about God's forgiveness, and to testify about God's compassion."*

You know when we arrived last Thursday, we had time, as what my son mentioned a while ago, to have a heart to heart talk with him. At that point my role was to be a facilitator, *"what do you want to say? Say it now, what do you want to tell?"* I asked them. I wanted that before Rod leaves, all the pains, all the bitterness, all the struggles, all the forgiveness that we can give in our hearts we can give him, we can give each other, and we can give to all the people who have become part of our family.

Nearing his end, while I fed him, sponge-bathed him, massaged him, I constantly whispered, *"Pa, I love you.. Pa, I love you."* How painful it was to swallow one's pride, to hug, to embrace, to care for the person, the very person who once hit you, kicked you and shouted bad and demeaning words at you. What can be more to that sacrifice? But I know it was by God's grace. It was by God's grace that I was able to do all of these. And until his very last breath, I held him in my very arms and before he breathed his last breath, we prayed together. I told him, *"Pa, please pray with me. Dear Jesus, please forgive me, please forgive us for all of our sins."* And that was his last.

That for me was the moment of real compassion and forgiveness. What more can surpass the compassion and forgiveness that God has given me and my children?

I repeat, our story, our life is a living testimony. Who would ever think that after eleven years, we are still here, united as one family? I know this is God's will that only Rod's death led to our final separation as husband and wife.

Ironically, a few months ago, our annulment was approved. My daughter asked me, *"Ma, are you happy?"* I answered, *"Anak, no!"* I cannot say that I was 100% happy because it was just on paper. But you know what I truly felt? I felt I got the justice that I deserved.

But God is all-knowing, He is so wise. God is so good that Rod died in my arms and in my son's arms. As my son said, all the eleven years lost with him were regained back in five days.

I sincerely thank all of you from the bottom of my heart. I thank Mommy, Ray, Marissa, Lola, uncles, aunties, all our cousins, because you were there to understand him during the eleven years that we were not together. God used you as his instruments to take care of him, you were the instruments used by God to make him feel that he is loved. Thank you so much. We will never be able to repay your generosity and kindness to Rod.

It all began with happiness, then struggles, then forgiveness, then compassion. Where does everything go back to? It's in love. Until now, that love is still in the hearts of each one. Come to think of it... come to think of it... nobody has ever imagined that everything has happened. But I believe, it was all by God's grace. And I can claim that we-- I, Rod, and our four children, are chosen by God to be examples, to be living witnesses of human love and of God's love.

Again, to all of you who love Rod - Pa, I have always told you that many people love you. I have repeatedly told him that. Now, maybe you have proven that I was right and I know he is really very happy. He is very happy that through this, a reunion has taken place. I am so delighted to see all the people who have become part of my life since Rod and I started. It's really a reunion. We will never forget this moment. Again, I thank all of you. Thank you very much.

TAGALOG

Unang una po sa lahat, nais ko pong magpasalamat. Ako po ay sobrang nagagalak na kayo po na nagmamahal kay Rod, kayo po na naging bahagi na ng kuwento naming mag-asawa simulat simula pa ay naririto ngayon upang sa ganon ay saksihan ang mga huling oras na makakasama natin siya.

Kagabi po ang shinare ko sa testimony ko ay binigyan ko ng title. Ngayon po ay uulitin ko yung sharing ko kagabi, not because I'm not prepared o wala akong masabi. Uulitin ko dahil sa ito ang buod ng aming kuwentong mag-asawa, ang aming kuwentong pamilya na nais kong ibahagi sa inyong lahat. Sana ang aming kasaysayan ay kapulutan natin lahat ng aral.

Ang aming paglalakbay bilang mag-asawa, nagkahiwalay, at nabuong muli ang aming pamilya. Ang sabi ko po kagabi, our story is a testimony of love, struggles, forgiveness and compassion.

Bakit po love? Bakit testimony of love? Kami po ni Rod ay nagsimula bilang mag boyfriend, masaya, sweet... andito sila uncle, sila lola, sila auntie, nakita po nila kung paano kami nagsimula. At nakita po nila na kami ay nangarap na makabuo ng isang napakasaya at napakagandang pamilya. Wala po ni isa sa aming dalawa ang nangarap o hinagip ng aming pangarap na magkaganito po kami, magkahiwalay kami. Wala po kaming hinangad kung hindi ang mapalaki at mabigyan ng maayos na kinabukasan ang mga bata at magkaroon ng simpleng buhay. Ang bawat sandali po ng aming pagsasama bilang mag boyfriend ng mahigit tatlong taon, bilang mag-asawa ng 10 or 11 years — lahat po ito ay punong-puno ng pagmamahal.

Opo! Struggles! Hindi naman po yun mawawala sa isang relasyon ang hindi pagkakaunawaan. Sabi ko nga po kagabi, kaming mag-asawa, ay nagmula sa magkaibang kasaysayan ng pamilya, may kanya-kanya po kaming katangian, may kanya-kanya kaming kahinaan na sinubukan naming pagusapan. Pagusapan sa mahinahon na paraan, humingi ng tulong kung kinakailangan. We tried to fight against all these weaknesses, and tried to be together as a happy family. Subalit sa hindi nga po inaasahan, yung kahinaan na yun ang kumain sa kawalan namin ng kakayanang magpatawad, walang kakayanang makinig sa bawat isa. Yun pong kahinaan na yun ang unti-unting kumain sa magandang relasyon na aming ipinundar.

Opo inaamin ko sa harap ninyong lahat, may kahinaan din po ako. And later on na-realize ko ano ba yung mga kahinaan kong yun? Napakarami! Subalit ang isa po sa kahinaan ko ay hindi po ako marunong lumaban, hindi po ako marunong mang-away, hindi po ako marunong sumigaw, hindi po ako marunong humingi ng tulong maski sa aking pamilya hanggat kaya ko, kinakaya ko. Yun po ang kahinaan ko na nitong bandang huli narealize ko. Si Rod, may mga kahinaan din po. Hindi ko na kailangang sabihin pa. Na hindi na namin ma patch up ang mga kahinaan na yun kaya sa bandang huli ay tumungo sa ganitong sitwasyon, na kami po ay maghiwalay.

Sabi po ng Ninang namin kanina, nakakalungkot lang kasi noong mga panahong iyon ay walang nangmatanda, walang mas matanda, walang mas mature, walang mas nakaka-unawa na tumulong sa amin upang maayos ang aming relasyon. Kaya unti-unti, we drifted apart.. we drifted apart.

Siguro po tinatanong niyo, sabi mo hindi ka marunong lumaban, sabi mo hindi ka marunong sumigaw, sabi mo hindi ka marunong whatever? Alam niyo po nung "kami," sinasabi ko pong "kami" dahil hindi lang po ako ang nagdesisyon para lumayo sa aking asawa. Kasama ko sa desisyon ang aking mga anak. Si Rocev noon ay batang bata pa. Subalit ako ay naniwala na sila ay may kakayanang magdesisyon kaya hindi ko lamang desisyon kundi desisyon naming lahat ang pag-alis.

Bakit ako nagdesisyon? Nagdesisyon po ako sa puntong malapit na pong mawala ang aking pinanghahawakang respeto sa sarili ko, malapit na pong mawala ang pinanghahawakan kong pagkatao. At bago po mawala sa akin iyon, minabuti kong ito na lang ang aking desisyon. Masakit. Struggle. Napakahirap po. Maaring hindi maunawaan ng lahat pero sa aking puso, at sa aking Panginoon alam ko na nauunawaan Niya ako.

Love. Struggles. Forgiveness. Sa loob po ng labing-isang taon na yun, tulad ng nasabi ng ninang namin, alam namin sa puso namin na mahal na mahal kami ng asawa ko. Kami din po sa tuwing kami ay magkakasama, walang panahon na hindi namin siya pinagu-usapan. "Ano na kaya nangyari sa papa niyo? Kumusta na kaya siya? Magaling na kaya siya?" Mahal natin ang papa niyo at paulit ulit ko pong sinasabi sa kanila na "anak huwag ninyong sisisihin ang papa niyo. Mahal na mahal kayo ng papa niyo subalit may kahinaan siya na hindi niya kayang i-express sa abot ng kanyang makakaya ang kanyang pagmamahal." Kaya po noong nagdesisyon kami noong March na puntahan siya, nung unang yakap ko pa lamang po sa kanya, naramdaman ko na, andun pa rin po ang pagmamahal. Noong yakapin siya ng aking mga anak, siguro nakita ng aking mga ka-facebook sa video, kitang kita, damang-dama ang forgiveness sa puso ng bawat isa. Alam niyo po paguwi naman tinanong ko ang mga anak ko, "anak ano ang naramdaman niyo?" Ang sabi po ng panganay ko nung pauwi na kami noong first time namin siyang puntahan, ang sabi niya, "Mama, para kaming nabunutan ng tinik." And it was true.

Yung forgiveness na iyon ang unti-unting nagbalik sa amin ng komunikasyon, ng constant kumustahan sa telepono at sa text, dahil alam po namin na ang kalooban ng Diyos ay para sa aming muli ang magkasama-sama.

Compassion. Nai-share ko na din po ito kagabi. Alam niyo po sa loob ng 4 o 5 araw na magkakasama kami, kasama ang mga bata, tinatanong ko ang sarili ko. Mabait ba talaga ako? Martir ba ako? O sadyang mapagpatawad ako? O sadyang ginagamit ako ng Panginoon para magmisyon? Para magbigay halimbawa sa mga katulad ko? Sa mga katulad kong maaring nakakaranas o nakaranas ng aking pinagdaanan? Kaya po minsan nabanggit ko sa mga bata, "alam niyo anak, ang paniwala ko talaga, we are chosen. Our family is chosen to testify about God's love, to testify about God's forgiveness, and to testify about God's compassion."

Alam niyo po noong pagbalik namin noong Thursday, nagkaroon ng panahon, sabi nga ng anak ko kanina, na magusap-usap bawat isa. Talagang ako at that point ang role ko was to be a facilitator, "sige anak ano ang gusto mong sabihin, ikaw ano ang gusto mong sabihin?" kasi po gusto kong bago umalis si Rod tungo sa kanyang pupuntahan, gusto kong lahat lahat, lahat ng sakit, lahat ng pait, all the pains, all the struggles, all the forgiveness that we can give in our hearts ay maibigay namin sa kanya, maibigay namin sa isat isa, at maibigay namin sa lahat ng mga taong naging bahagi ng kasaysayan namin bilang pamilya.

In the end sinusubuan ko siya, sponge bath ko siya, hinihimas, at lagi ko pong binubulungan, "Pa, I love you.. Pa, I love you." Gaanong sakit, gaanong paglunok sa pride or whatever you call it ang muling yakapin, yakapin ang tao, ang isang tao na minsan sa buhay mo ay nanapak sayo? Na tumadyak sayo? Na nagmura sayo? Gaanong sakripisyo po yun? But I know it was by God's grace. It was by God's grace na nagawa ko po iyon. At sa huling sandali ng kanyang hininga, hawak hawak ko po siya, bago siya lagutan ng kanyang huling hininga, nagdasal po kami. Sabi ko po sa kanya, "Pa, please pray with me. Dear Jesus, patawarin niyo na po ako, patawarin niyo na po kami sa aming mga pagkakasala." And that was his last breath.

That for me was the moment of real compassion and forgiveness. Anong hihigit pa? Anong hihigit pa sa compassion and forgiveness that God has given me and my children?

Ulitin ko po. Our story, our life is a living testimony. Biruin mo, sino ang maga-akalang after 11 years, andito parin kami, buo. Alam kong kalooban ng Diyos na hanggang sa bandang huli, kami ay maghihiwalay na sa mata ng Diyos ay mag-asawa pa rin kami.

A few months ago, na-approve yung annulment namin. Sabi ng anak ko, "Ma. Masaya ka ba?" sabi ko "Anak, hindi." I cannot say na I am 100% happy kasi papel lang yun eh. But you know kung ano ang naramdaman ko? I felt I got the justice that I deserved.

Pero marunong ang Diyos, napakarunong Niya. God is so good that he died in my arms and in my son's arms. Yung sabi ng anak ko kanina, yung labing isang taon na iyon ay nasulit, nasulit po in just 5 days.

Ako po ay nagpapasalamat, from the bottom of my heart. Ako ay nagpapasalamat kay Mommy, kay Ray, kay Marissa, kina lola, kina uncle, kina auntie, sa lahat ng mga pinsan because you were there to understand him during the 11 years that we were not together. God used you as his instruments to take care of him, kayo po yung instrumentong nagparamdam sa kanya na may nagmamahal sa kanya. Maraming maraming salamat. Hindi po namin masusuklian ang inyong kabutihang loob na inyo pong ibinigay kay Rod.

Nagsimula sa maganda, nagkaroon ng struggles, nagkaroon ng forgiveness, nagkaroon ng compassion. Saan bumalik iyon?

It's in love. Hanggang ngayon po andun ang pagmamahal sa bawat isa. Nakakatuwang isipin… nakakatuwang isipin, pero hindi mo ma-imagine kung paano nangyari ang lahat. But I believe it was all by God's grace. And I can claim, kami – ako, si Rod, ang aking apat na anak, ay pinili ng Diyos upang maging halimbawa, upang maging buhay na patotoo ng pag-ibig, pagmamahal, at pag-ibig ng Diyos.

Muli po sa inyong lahat na nagmamahal sa kanya, Pa, lagi kong sinasabi sa iyo, marami ang nagmamahal sa iyo. Pauli-ulit ko pong sinasabi sa kanya iyan. Ngayon siguro na-prove na niya and he is really very happy. Tuwang –tuwa po siya na ang pangyayaring ito ay naging reunion. Ako po ay natutuwa na nakita ko pong lahat ang mga taong naging bahagi ng buhay ko simula po nang aming pagiging mag-asawa. It's really a reunion. So, itong sandali pong ito ay hinding hindi namin makakalimutan. Muli, ako po ay nagpapasalamat sa inyong lahat. Maraming salamat po.

LET US PRAY…

Forgiving Lord, thank you for giving me enormous courage and strength that finally after long years of pain, I was able to forgive and be healed, that I was able to verbally share them. The opportunity you have given me to spend the last few days with him before he joined You was a great blessing. Continue anointing me that I may be a living witness of how forgiving, loving, and compassionate God you are. Amen.

POINTS TO PONDER...

1. Is there someone you have difficulty forgiving? What has he/she done to you?

2. Do you have any plans of mending your broken relationship with that person?

3. What possible helps do you need to be reconciled with him/her?

TALK TO GOD...

____

____

____

____

____

____

____

____

____

3 FORGIVENESS

"Let all bitterness and wrath and anger and clamor and
slander be put away from you,
along with all malice.
Be kind to one another, tenderhearted,
forgiving one another,
as God in Christ forgave you.
Ephesians 4:31-32

ONE SATURDAY MORNING in June 2013 over breakfast, one of my dear friends unexpectedly asked the question. *"How was your relationship with your husband? Can you tell me about it?"* I wondered why she asked me the question. I have shared a bit of my past with her but not in detail considering that we still didn't know each other very well. But I ended telling her my whole story.

I narrated how we started with a happy marriage. *"We were classmates in Law school and after more than three years of being boyfriend and girlfriend, we decided to get married. My sisters envied me because my husband did the household chores, he took care of our children, and never made me do the laundry. My students and co-teachers in my former school saw us as a sweet couple. We supported each other in our career. He used to bring and pick me up from graduate school."* Thus, I started recounting our happy days together.

"But later on problems came that strained our relationship and the family. These eventually led to our separation. In the beginning, we were able to settle the issues and managed to work things out together. However, everything just went out of our control. He began to be very violent. I've received all kinds of bad words, slapping, hitting, kicking, punching, and shouting- I was a battered wife. And I attributed all of this to his psychological and mental condition. He was diagnosed with manic depression or bipolar disorder. This was aggravated with his degenerating health condition—diabetes which was quite serious." I narrated.

"Have you forgiven him?" she asked. Proudly I said, *"Sure! I have definitely forgiven him long time ago."* I insisted. *"Are you sure you have forgiven him?"* She once again asked. This time, I began to reflect and ask myself the same question, *"Have I really and truly forgiven him?"*

"Did you ever have any chance to talk to him since then? Did you ever visit him? She asked. *"No!"* I said. *"I'm scared. He might hurt me again. I know, and I have been telling my children that time will come when we will see him again. I know it will come. But I'm not sure when will that*

time come. I want to see him when he will be very weak so that he could not even lift his arms to hurt or hit me or my children. "I started to break in tears. The whole experience flashed into my memory. And I was so frightened… Really frightened.

"You know, your husband loves you and your children so much. He is missing you a lot. But he is suffering. He is very weak now and he needs you. He needs your forgiveness. He is waiting for you," my friend said. When I heard this, I felt God talking to me. As if it was God telling me that the forgiveness I have been claiming for my husband was only superficial. I felt God leading me and inviting me to go and reach out to him.

"You know what he is going through is not easy." It was my friend again. *"For all you know this is not what he wants, he wants his family to be together but he has lost control of everything. He must have regretted everything that he has done but there is no way for him to win you and your children back. Don't you realize the difficulty he is going through?"*

I was deeply troubled after that. We spent the whole day talking. I poured out all the pent-up anger and emotions that I have kept in my heart all these years. All the pains that I have buried, I dug them out. The tears started to fall as I cried out my hurt feelings. It was a catharsis.

My friend embraced me tightly and I felt it was God embracing me, accepting me wholeheartedly, without any pretension, with forgiveness and compassion. God was telling me, *"Emely, my child, I know you have forgiven him but it's not enough.*

You have to do more. You have to make him feel your and your children's forgiveness for him. He needs that. Let him rest... let him rest." I had goose bumps having these realizations.

I spent the rest of the day praying with my friend. *"What shall I do?"* I asked myself. I was not ready to see him. Not yet. Not soon. My friend encouraged me to face reality. She assured me that if ever we decide to see him everything will be all right. Just have faith and trust in God.

She also reminded me that maybe that is the reason why after many years my annulment has not yet been approved. *"Remember, what God has united, no man can separate?"* She reminded me. I agreed. *"The Lord loves you that He wants everything to take its normal course."* I again agreed.

It was a sleepless night I had. I seemed to hear his voice saying *"Ma, patawarin mo ako. Mahal na mahal kita."* **(Ma, please forgive me. I love you very much.)** It felt so real. I felt his presence right beside me, begging for my forgiveness. I prayed so hard. *"Dear Lord, if this is a wake-up call for me to be more humble and reach out to him, yes, I will. If this will give him peace, I will."*

Meeting him personally was just impossible at that time. Or perhaps my heart was not really ready to see him. An idea came into my mind. It was a few days before his birthday and so writing him would be a good idea. I talked to my children and convinced them to visit my husband. But they refused. So, I explained further that this is a good way of making him feel that despite everything that have happened he is still their father and to make him feel we have forgiven him. I also told them that if something happens to him, we did our part. Since the children refused to see him, we decided to write him a letter. Convinced with what we were going to do, my children wrote him.

The following were my and my children's letters:

Happy birthday po. Kamusta na po kayo? I hope you're doing well. Sana po hindi ninyo nakakalimutang magpray para po magthank you kay Lord sa mga blessings na natatanggap ninyo araw-araw.

Happy Birthday! How are you? I hope you're doing well. I hope that you have not forgotten to pray and thank God for all the blessings you have received everyday.

Madami nang years yung nagdaan na hindi kita nababati para sa birthday mo Pa, pero hindi ko yun nakakalimutan. Tulad ngayon. Pa, sana malaman mo na love ka pa din namin kahit na ano man yung nangyari in the past. Hindi ko nakakalimutan na ikaw pa din ang papa namin. Kahit na anong mangyari, proud pa din ako kasi I am your daughter.

Many years have passed that I have failed to greet you Happy Birthday, Pa, but I have never forgotten that. Like now, Pa, I want you to know that we still love you despite what happened in the past. I have never forgotten that you are still our father. Despite everything that happened, I am still proud to be your daughter.

Happy happy birthday pa, I love you. Sana okay ka lang palagi. Hindi ka po nawawala sa prayers ko.

Happy happy birthday, Pa. I love you. I hope you are always okay. You are always in my prayers.

Love, Renz

Unang una po sa lahat, happy birthday. Another year has been given to you to live. Kamusta na po kayo? Sobrang tagal na po since the last time we talked. But i hope you're okay. Ako po, eto mag third year college na. Mahirap po pero kinakaya and kakayanin para in the near future, i'd be able to stand tall and help Mama. Ano naman pong pinagkakaabalahan nyo ngayon? Ako po, may summer classes, sobrang busy po kasi maraming projects and activities eh limited po ung time.

First of all, Happy birthday! Another year has been given to you to live. How are you? It's been so long since the last time we talked. But I hope you're okay. As for me, I am already in 3rd year college. It is difficult but I am trying and must try my best so that in the future I'd be able to stand tall and help Mama. What's keeping you busy these days? I am busy with my summer classes, so busy because I have a lot of projects and limited time.

Gusto ko pong malaman nyo na kahit hindi na po tayo magkasama, hindi ko po nalilimutang isipin kayo, kung kamusta kayo, anong nangyayari sa inyo. Kasi po para sakin, part pa rin po kayo ng family ko and ng buhay ko. Kasi without you, baka wala rin ako ngayon. I just want you to know that wherever you are, whatever you're doing, i still consider you as part of the family.

I want you to know that even though we are living separately, I never fail to think about you, how you are doing, and what is happening with you. Because for me, you are still part of the family and my life. Because without you, I am not in this world. I just want you to know that wherever you are, whatever you're doing, i still consider you as part of the family.

Happy birthday po. Enjoy nyo po birthday niyo. God bless!

Happy birthday. Enjoy your birthday. God bless!

Kelly

Hello Papa! HAPPY BIRTHDAY PO!! More birthdays to come Pa!

Kamusta na Pa? Sana po ay okay ka lang. Okay lang naman po kaming magkakapatid. Si Ate Renz graduating na po sa pasukan. Si Ate Kelly 3rd year college na po sa pasukan. Si Rocev naman po, kagagraduate lang ng elementary, high school na sa pasukan. Binatang-binata na nga eh. Tas ako naman Pa, kagagraduate ko lang din

po ng high school. Nagtapos po akong Valedictorian ng St. Mary's Seminary. Si Mama naman ay nagtatrabaho sa ibang bansa. Isa siyang OFW Pa. Pero kahit magkakalayo kami, masaya naman kami kahit papaano.

How are you, Pa? I hope you are okay. I and my siblings are okay. Ate Renz is graduating next year. Ate Kelly will be in 3rd year. Rocev just graduated from elementary. He will be in high school next year. He is now a big boy. Then as for me, I just graduated from high school. I graduated Valedictorian at the St. Marys Seminary. Mama is working abroad. She is an OFW. But even if we are far from each other, we are happy.

Sobrang bilis ng panahon Pa. Kailan lang nung uhuging mga bata lang kami. Parang kailan lang nung laro palagi ang nasa isip namin. Ngayon ay may mga isip na kami. Malalaki na kami Pa. Matagal na rin nung huli kitang nakita Pa. Maliit pa ako noon pero alam ko kung sino ka Pa. Alam kong mahal mo kami. Siguro ay hindi mo lang mai-express ng maayos ito sa amin. Sa totoo lang Pa there are times na kailangan ka namin kasi alam kong hirap na hirap na si Mama pero wala naman kaming magagawa kundi magtiis.

Time flies so fast, Pa. We were just small kids then, when all we were thinking was about playing. But now, we are grown-ups already. It's been long since I last met you. I was still young but I know who you are, Pa. I know that you love us. Maybe you just don't know how to express this love to us. Honestly Pa, there are times when we need you here with us because I know Mama is having such a difficulty but we cannot do anything but endure.

Papa, alagaan mo health mo. Wag mong papabayaan sarili mo. Mag-iingat ka po lagi. Kahit ano po ang mangyari, wag mo kakalimutang magdasal Pa. Si God lang ang laging nasa tabi nating lahat. Pray for us and most especially for yourself.

Papa, take care of your health. Don't neglect yourself. Take care always. Whatever happens, don't forget to pray, Pa. Only God is always at our side. Pray for us and especially for yourself.

Hanggang dito na lang Pa. Ingat ka lagi. I love you!

Till then, Pa. Take care always. I love you!

Reinier

Happy Birthday nga po pala. Musta ka naman po? Ok ka lang ba jan? Natatandaan mo po ba ako? Ako yung bunso niyo. Si Rocev. Masaya po ba kayo na wala kami sa inyo? Hehe

Happy birthday! How are you? Are you okay? Do you still remember me? I am Rocev. Are you happy that we are not with you? Hehe!

Masarap po ba yung feeling na lumaki ka ng walang naggagabay na ama saiyo? Diba po hindi? Pero kinaya ko kasi meron akong nanay na tumatayo ko ring tatay sa araw-

araw kong pangangailangan. Salamat po dahil kahit papano ay hindi niyo po kami naisipang hanapin at kausapin. Kahit papano po. Meron parin akong unting natitirang pagmamahal sa inyo.

Does it feel good to grow up without a father guiding you? It doesn't, right? But I did it because I have a mother who is at the same time my father who attends to my everyday needs. Thank you that you did not look for us or talk to us anymore. Despite everything, I still love you.

Ang iyong bunso, *(Your youngest)*

Rocev

How are you?

We decided to write you to let you know that we still remember you especially on your birthday. Happy birthday!

As I promised you, I will never ever neglect the children. Thank GOD that with His guidance and grace they are growing to be mature and smart kids. They are all grown-ups. And I'm proud to say that they are all doing great in their academics and in their personal lives. They are very responsible and independent kids.

Renz is graduating next year sa UPLB. She's turning 21 this year. She was supposed to graduate this March but she was an exchange student for a year in Catholic University of Korea so she was delayed for one year. She's now doing her OJT. Development Communication is her major. She's very active in school activities, too.

Racquel will be 3rd year in June at UPLB also. She is a debater. She has been joining national debate competitions and she had been winning. She's also very active in school activities. Human Ecology is her major. She'll be turning 18 soon.

Reinier just graduated Valedictorian this March at Saint Mary's Seminary. He was such a great blessing because he is the one always praying for us. He will be entering college this June and he will be turning 16 a few days from now.

Rocev is a very smart, sweet, charming boy. He lived with me in Korea for more than a year. He studied for a year here. He just finished Grade VI. In June, he will be Grade VII. He graduated 2nd Honorable Mention and will be turning 13 this year.

I want you to be proud of them because they are your kids. Look at their pictures… thank GOD he guided us all these years. He has provided everything we need. Knowing what your kids have become…I hope you will be at peace. I promise I will take care of them….

Emely

After sending those letters I felt better. And I told God, if anything happens we did our part.

At this point, the Spirit was still leading me to see him, to talk to him personally. I've heard that his physical condition was getting worse by the day so I and my children were planning to really see him soon. I fervently prayed for that day that God may guide us, so we be able to fulfill his commandment to "put away all bitterness, wrath, anger, clamor, slander, and malice. Let kindness, tenderheartedness, and forgiveness reign."

LET US PRAY...

I'm sorry, Lord, that all those years I have confessed, "yes I have forgiven him," but in reality I have not, for I refused to personally embrace him. Thank you for sending me your instruments to make me realize a big omission of my duty as your child. I pray, dear Lord, that you grant me the courage to testify for God not only through lip service but by deeds. AMEN.

POINTS TO PONDER...

1. How many times have you said you've forgiven someone, or everything is okay, but actually you have/are not? In what situations?
2. Do you exert some effort to discuss your differences with someone?
3. How do you resolve personal grudges or issues with someone?

TALK TO GOD...

____

____

____

____

4 COMPASSION

Therefore, as God's chosen people, holy and dearly loved,
clothe yourselves with compassion, kindness, humility,
gentleness and patience. Bear with each other and forgive one
another if any of you has a grievance against someone. Forgive
as the Lord forgave you. And over all these virtues put on love
which binds them all together in perfect unity. Let the peace of
Christ rule in your hearts, since as members of one body you
were called to peace.
And be thankful.
Colossians 3:12-15

AFTER SENDING THE LETTERS, it took me and
my children almost nine months to prepare ourselves to
see my husband personally. Every time I'd go home for
vacation, we would plan visiting him but we never had the
courage to actually go, or perhaps we were not yet ready
to face him. We finally agreed to see him in April, after
my eldest daughter's graduation.

I came back to Korea at the end of February for the opening of the Spring Semester. One day at about 9:00 in the morning, upon waking up, I saw my husband sitting at the corner of my bed looking at me. I don't know if it was my sixth sense at work, but I quickly closed my eyes. I couldn't believe what I saw. So, I prayed. I prayed so hard and asked myself, "What does this mean? Is the Lord telling me something? What does God want me to do?"

I was stunned for quite a while. Honestly, I was not scared of what I saw but I was scared of what I was supposed to do next. *This is it!* I told myself. "We must see him. This might be a sign for me and my children to finally go and meet him." At that moment, I decided to go home to the Philippines. But something came up that held my decision back. I cancelled my plan.

The whole week passed with that image of my husband 'looking at me' remained constant in my mind. I was bothered. I shared this with my friend and she said, *"Why should you worry about what he and his relatives will say? If you are doing it in faith, and you know that what you are doing is good, nothing will go wrong. God will be with you all the way. This is your chance to express the pent-up emotions and resentments you have inside. You need to free yourself from those emotions."* That encouragement convinced me and finally I booked my ticket.

No one in my family knew about my plan. Nobody knew I was going home. On my way to Los Banos, I texted my children and they were all surprised. They were all wondering why I went home without informing them. I told them to wait for me and I will discuss something very important to them.

That night, I talked to my brother, my sister and children. I narrated my experience and that I felt it was time for us to see him. I told them that his diabetes was getting worse and his health was deteriorating so maybe it was necessary to talk to him so that if anything happens we are all at peace. Everyone agreed.

The next day, my brother drove us to Tarlac and there we met my youngest son from Ilocos with his cousin. Some of our family friends were with us and they constantly were praying for us. While we were traveling I kept on praying and telling God, *"Lord, please guide us. I know we are doing the right thing so please protect us. These arms…these arms Oh, Lord are here for a reason. Whatever he does to me, I will just embrace him because these are what my arms are made for."*

While nearing their house, my children noticed some men around and they began to be scared. My youngest son expressed, *"Ma, I'm scared!"* *"Don't be scared. For as long as Mama is here, nothing wrong will happen."* I assured him. My brother started to feel nervous with what he heard. My daughter said, *"Ma, you be the first one to get off the car."* *"Sure!"* I said without hesitation. Honestly, I was also scared, but I had to be strong for my children.

From a distance, I could see my husband standing while he was trying to recognize who were coming. *"There is your Papa!"* I told my children. The nervousness and tension escalated. When the car stopped, I immediately got down the car. Upon recognizing me he shouted saying *"Putangina (Fuck) Ma!"* I ran to him and not minding what his words meant, whether he was angry or surprised, I threw my arms around him and hugged him tightly. He hugged me in return and he started to cry. He whispered, *"Ma, patawarin mo ako sa lahat ng aking mga pagkukulang sa iyo at sa mga bata. Patawarin mo ako. Mahal ko kayo,"* **(Ma, please forgive me from all of my shortcomings. Please forgive me. I love you all)** he was sobbing. I called my children and they too, embraced their father. He repeatedly said sorry to his children.

This was the moment of total forgiveness. After ten long years of separation, of keeping all the pain and hurt inside us, the bad memories in our minds, we have finally come to terms with ourselves and with him. This was the moment of compassion, kindness, humility, gentleness and patience. This was the very moment when God made His presence felt deeply and concretely by everyone. My husband said, *"Puwede na akong mamatay, nakita ko na kayo"* **(I can die anytime because I have already seen you).**

After that, I held his face, stared at him and looked at him in the eyes. I ran out of words. The anger, the pain and the resentments were all gone. I couldn't believe how his face has gone so thin and dark. He couldn't walk straight anymore without his cane. His feet were swollen. And his hands…. His hands caught my attention. I used to pray, *"Lord, when we see him, I hope he would not have that power to lift his hands to hit or to hurt us anymore."* True enough. He had this big, open, fresh wound on his hand, his fingers were twisted, and as he said he could not even hold a pen or write anymore. The funny thing though, is that he can still hold a cigar.

I gave him and the children time to talk. They talked about the happy memories they had in childhood. They remembered eating at Jollibee, watching movies, going to the malls, and others. My children told him about what is happening with them in school. My husband was happy. He was proud of what his children have become. I ran out of words to describe my feelings at that instant. It was peace – an indescribable peace and joy in my heart.

Visit to Rod after 10 years of separation. It was the moment of forgiveness and reconciliation.

When my mother-in-law came home, we greeted her and showed her the respect accorded to an in-law. I did not say anything about the past. We just talked about the present. She said she was happy that God heard her prayers. *"I have been praying for this,"* she said with teary eyes.

It was an instant reunion. My brother-in-law and sister-in-law came with their children. Our children were still small when they met each other. Now, they are all grown-ups and happy to finally meet their cousins.

We left their house with light, clean, and pure hearts. My children said they pity him because of his physical condition. I told them to continue praying for him because it is the only thing we can do for him. He needs prayers. My children, without hesitation, agreed with my suggestion.

My nephew, Glenn Mark, showed us a video he took, without us knowing it, of **"that moment!"** While watching, I cannot even imagine how we did it. I, myself was inspired when I saw it. I wanted to share it with my friends, not because I wanted to show off what I did, but I wanted them to be inspired and be challenged as well. If I was able to do it, so they can, too. Here's the link to the video:

http://www.youtube.com/watch?v=O8c-UkaYybM

One of the messages I got from a colleague after she watched the video was, *"I can't help but ask you this? Tao ka ba talaga mam? Anghel ka naman yata talaga eh… pinadala ka ni Lord to inspire thousands of pipol, kilala mo man o hindi. Saludo ako sayo mam!!!* **(Are you really a human being? I think you are an angel. God sent you to inspire thousands of people, whether you know them or not. I salute you, Ma'am!!!)** *You deserve everything…"*

As I have consistently answered those who have been asking how I survived all these ordeals in my life, my answer is, *"It was by God's grace! It was God who made all these possible. Of course through the help of people, my family and friends, whom He constantly sent to assist me and my children."* The challenge of forgiving someone, embracing him and accepting him again, forgetting the pain and starting anew is the very essence of God's commandment, *"Love one another!"*

One of my friends keeps on telling me, *"You and your children are chosen by God to spread his love on earth. To be an inspiration to others."* Every time she tells me this, I feel so humbled and unworthy. But yes, I do believe, my family is chosen and dearly loved by God. Therefore He clothed us with compassion, kindness, gentleness and patience. That is why we were able to forgive as the Lord has forgiven us. It is love that binds us together in perfect unity. So, in prayer, I say, *"Let the peace of Christ rule in our hearts, since as members of one body we were called in peace. Amen!"*

LET US PRAY...

Compassionate God, what I and my children went through was not at all easy. But thank you for guiding us all the way. Thank you for working the miracle of forgiveness in our hearts possible. Human as we are, it was a great challenge, but you made it easier for us. Thank you for saving us from guilt that we could have carried in our hearts for the rest of our lives. Continue using me and my children as your living witnesses of your unconditional love. AMEN.

POINTS TO PONDER...

1. Have you honestly asked God to help you forgive someone who might have caused you pain?
2. Are you ready to let God be in total control of how you are feeling and allowing him to perform a miracle in your life?
3. Are you ready to love again and be totally healed before it's too late?

TALK TO GOD...

____

____

____

____

____

____

5 PRAYER WORKS

> "And the prayer of faith shall save the sick,
> and the Lord shall raise him up;
> and if he has committed sins,
> they shall be forgiven him."
> James 5:15

NOVEMBER 2, 2014, after the Sunday Mass, I sent Rod a message and asked him how he was doing and reminded him that Renz had her birthday yesterday. I also asked him if he greeted her. He answered yes. He also mentioned that his health condition was getting worse. He added, *"I hope you are happy now that you already got what you wanted."*Oooopppsssss!!! This reply got me into saying, *"here we go again!"*

This response from him sparked a whole day of exchanging painful text messages, outpouring of emotions, expressing negative sentiments, resentments and blames thrown to each other for everything that has happened in the past that caused our marital breakdown, the family separation, his present situation, to almost everything.

When I and my children decided to see him last March 2014, I chose not to talk about the past anymore. I did not want to dig deep into the painful memories buried 10-11 years ago. I thought it was better not to talk about it, easier for us to forgive and forget.

But the exchange of messages prompted me to answer back, to defend myself and my children from his judgments, and express what I honestly and truly felt with everything that happened. I could no longer control myself from telling him all the pent-up emotions in my heart. I told myself, *"Yes, maybe this is the moment for me to express myself. Once and for all, this is my turn to fight for myself and assert myself."* In the end, I felt better. It was such a relief to express my feelings. I realized keeping quiet and not making him know how I felt was not helpful at all. Alas!! I felt liberated! I felt free from pains and bad memories.

He expressed his disappointments as well. He showed his depression, and his lack of faith and humility to come before the Lord and repent.

He said, *"Huwag sana kayong magagalit mam pero dalawa pala ang master sa mundong ibabaw hindi lang ang cristo na kinikilala niyo....wala ng magagawa ang Diyos dito ... pinahihirapan niya ako.*

Halos sampung taon akong nagsimba at nagpray sa kanya, wala po palang kuwenta yun. Nagsayang lang pala ako mam. Pinabayaan lang niya ako. I'm sorry sa inyong lahat pero hindi ako hihingi ng tawad sa Diyos na nagpahirap sa akin. Naiyak ako sa dasal mo mam pero hindi na ako naniniwala sa kanya. Hinila niya ako pababa wala siyang kuwenta sa kabila ng pagsimba at prayers ko." **(Don't get angry Ma'am, but I realized there are two masters in this world, it's not only the Christ that you know….God cannot do anything here anymore… he is making me suffer. For almost ten years I went to church and I prayed but everything was useless. I just wasted my time, Ma'am. He abandoned me. I am sorry to all of you but I will not ask forgiveness from God who made me suffer. Your prayer made me cry, Ma'am but I don't believe in him anymore. He pulled me down. He is useless, despite my going to church and all my prayers.)**

Reading these messages from him caused me mixed emotions and reactions. At first I was mad at him. I was angry because I could not understand why he could not just be humble before the Lord and ask for compassion and forgiveness. However, I also felt sad for him because after ten years, how can he not realize that the Lord has given him all the chances and opportunities to repent, how can he not feel the love of God. I could not really understand.

My text messages were prayers. At that point in time I realized that I have exhausted all my efforts to help him and any word I tell him will only be useless and the more he would defend himself negatively. I realized at that time that the only thing I can do was to bend my knees and ask for divine intervention, to allow God's compassion and power to just move, for in my heart, I knew and I believed that God's power is mightier than any other power in this world.

I cried… I cried a lot in the silence of my room. But those tears were said in prayer. For me, it was an indescribable suffering for him, for his lack of faith, for his lack of humility before the Lord.

All throughout that week, I made hundreds of prayer requests from my friends, my children and my family. From the time I woke up in the morning, while having meals, while walking, in my silence, all I said were prayers for him- *"Lord, have mercy on him."* I offered everything I did during that week for his conversion and for acceptance of God's love. My prayer to the divine mercy was countless, and with those prayers was my faith that He, indeed, will forgive him and heal him.

Prayers move mountains! Yes, it really does!

Friday, November 7, 2014, a few days after that painful, emotional, and confrontational exchange of text messages, I received another message from him. He asked, *"mahal niyo pa ba ako?"* **(Do you still love me?)** I answered, *"Opo. Mahal na mahal na mahal."* **(Yes, we love you very much.)** He replied, *"Ma, I'm like Thomas. I don't know what to follow, my heart or my head."*

"Yes! The spirit is at work! God's mercy is at work!" I immediately answered him, *"Follow your heart because your heart will lead you to the truth. In your heart there is God. And in God there is peace. And in peace there is love."* He answered back, *"Tama ka. Kung may pera lang ako pinauwi na kita para magusap-usap na tayo. Iba na ang pakiramdam ko."* **(You're right. If only I have money I could have asked you to go home so that we can talk. I'm having a strange feeling.)** At that very instant, I said a prayer of thanksgiving to God. *"Dear Lord, thank you. Thank you for touching his heart, thank you for your mercy."* I continued praying for him everyday. I continued asking my friends to pray for him.

Wednesday, November 12, 2014 at around 12 noon, I received another text message from him. He said, *"Ma, asap."* I asked, *"Ang alin?"* **(which one?)** He said, *"Ma, I'm dying na."* **(Ma, I'm dying.)** I answered, *"Pa, intayin mo kami ng mga anak mo. Hold on, ok? Dadating kami."* **(Pa, wait for me and your children. Hold on, OK?)**

At that very instant, I asked one of my friends for help to book my ticket going back home. That very same day, I flew back to the Philippines and proceeded to Tarlac with my children to see him. It was a tearful moment for our family that was finally reunited. But it was the most liberating and freeing moment in our lives as well.

A few hours after we have talked, he passed out. His blood sugar dropped to 41 and we thought he was leaving us at that moment. But thank God, he was still given a few days to be with us. He underwent dialysis for the first time that same day. After his dialysis, we looked for a priest to give him the Sacrament of the Anointing of the Sick.

He seemed to look better after that. He spent quality time with the children and he was happy watching them. Renz, Racquel, and Rocev had to go back to Los Banos with my brother because they already missed their classes for two days. He gave his permission for them to leave. That night, he and Reinier spent time together.

Our last family picture before Rod joined the Creator. This was taken before Renz, Racquel, and Rocev left for Los Baños with my brother, Tante.

The following day, November 17, 2014 at around 3:30 in the morning, I was seated beside him, watching him while he was asleep. I prayed repeatedly the Rosary of the Chaplet of the Divine Mercy. Offering every prayer of *"Lord, have mercy on Rod and of the whole world,"* for his forgiveness and compassion. He was shivering while sleeping. He could not control his reflexes anymore.

At around 4:30 he woke up and asked for a cup of coffee and "pandesal." We had coffee together that morning. Little did I know that it was our last coffee together.

At around 5:30 he started to feel uneasy. I continued praying and encouraged him to pray with me. He agreed. He started complaining about feeling hot, then feeling cold, having stomach ache, pains all over his body. He started coughing, his phlegm looked reddish. I was worried but I did not tell him. I woke my son up to help me because I was already having difficulty taking care of him by myself. My son woke up and he helped me. We managed to bring him to the restroom twice.

While he was in pain, we continued praying. My son and I whispered *"I love you"* to him. Hugging him I said, *"Pa, let's pray… let's pray together."* I knew he did, I knew he prayed with me and my son. But at that moment, I also felt that the devil was at work. I heard him saying *"Putangina"* **(Fuck!)** so I started casting out and loudly I said, *"In Jesus' name, leave him. Lord, please send your angels to bring him to heaven! Please Lord."*

My son and I were already holding him by the head. We were both crying and after casting out, my husband took a deep breath. Again, I shouted while crying, *"Pa. please pray with me. Let's pray together. Dear Jesus, patawarin niyo na po ako sa aking mga kasalanan. Lord, please patawarin niyo na po kami.'* **(Dear Jesus, forgive me from all of my sins. Lord, please forgive us.)** *Lord, have mercy, Lord. Have mercy."* After praying this, he vomited blood, took a deep breath, and while looking at me and my son, he slowly closed his eyes.

The most wonderful experience I and my son had at that very moment was that he died in our very arms. My son was at his right and I was at his left. We struggled with him while he fought for his life, we prayed together, we witnessed his conversion, and we saw him close his eyes.

I felt peace after that. I seemed to hear the angels from heaven rejoicing and singing because he finally surrendered his very life to God. I felt the angels come down, fetched him, and brought him to heaven, in our Father's home. I know he is now at peace with God, he is watching over us, and he has been praying for us.

Prayers can soften a hardened heart! God's mercy can save us from our wickedness and sinfulness! Prayers turn the impossible to possible. Prayers really work! Indeed, the prayers of His faithful people can heal the sick and forgive the sins others have committed. For all our friends who prayed for him, and prayed with us, our heartfelt thanks. May God, in his abundance, bless you all.

LET US PRAY...

Ever forgiving God, thank you for giving Rod a chance to repent before he joined you. Thank you for making his conversion possible and for making your power reveal that you have indeed softened a hardened heart. Your mercy is immense that no evil can overpower it. Thank you also for giving me a very strong and understanding heart that I was able to journey with him, even to the last moment, in his journey to conversion. May you continue to bless me so that I may share your miracle to every person I meet. AMEN.

POINTS TO PONDER...

1. Have you ever witnessed a dying person, especially someone close to you? How did you manage it?
2. How would you probably talk to a person close to you who does not believe in God and blames Him for his misfortune?
3. What about you? Have you ever questioned God when you are suffering or any problem comes to you?

TALK TO GOD...

____

____

____

____

6 LOVE IS LOVE

"If you love someone,
there's nothing you can do but to return to him."
Reinier Josef D. Abagat

This was Reinier's, eulogy during the wake. The first part is the English translation and the second part is the Tagalog version (verbatim). You can watch the video on this link:

https://www.youtube.com/watch?v=O-MH3rUSArQ

ENGLISH

ME AND MY FATHER LIVED SEPARATELY for eleven years. And in all these years, there was just one thing that I felt. I terribly missed him. Yet, I cannot do anything but to pray. I always prayed that he was okay

because I knew he was sick. I prayed that he was okay and that somebody was taking care of him.

So, we decided to see him. Mama sent us a message saying, *"Anak, let's visit Papa. He is dying."* So, I immediately prayed and said, *"Lord, no! Please! I want to be with Papa for a longer time."*

So, when we were in the hospital, we had a chance to have a heart to heart talk as a family. We were able to express everything that was buried in our hearts for a long time. I told Papa, *"Papa you know, all these years, every Christmas, I only had one wish. I wished that we will be together as a family. I prayed for this for eleven years but my prayer was never granted."* Papa answered, *"Anak, I promise you, this Christmas, we will all be together."* So, I expected it to happen because that was my wish. He added, *"Anak, I will fight for us, for our family."* When Papa said that, I really expected it to happen.

I terribly missed him and in the four days that we were with him, in my case five days because I was there on the day he died, all the days lost were redeemed. That's why I thank God that we were given a chance to be together even for a short while. Those days that I've been longing for as a son came true as we were able to share stories about our favorites--wrestling, basketball, and girls. We shared a lot of stories. That was what I missed most--to have a father to talk with. Yet, in the five days I spent with him, the years lost were all redeemed. That's why I thank the Lord so much.

So, on his last day, at around 6 o'clock in the morning, mama woke me up. It was my first time to wake up without being forced. One yell and I was awake. *"Anak, wake up,"* Mama said. When I looked at Papa I stood up immediately. Papa was already pale. I saw Mama was in so much difficulty. Papa was uneasy. He did not know what position to take. I also felt Papa was struggling and suffering. So, what Mama did that morning was she turned on the laptop and she played a prayer. We prayed and prayed all throughout.

But this is the funny part. From time to time the nurse would come and give some prescriptions. Mama would leave me because she needed to go down to the pharmacy. Every time she leaves me, I would hold Papa's hand. I prayed, *"Lord, no! I cannot bear this alone."* Twice Mama had to go down and buy some medicines for Papa.

That very moment, Papa perhaps felt that his time has come. He positioned himself on the bed, stretched his legs, and breathed his last breath. Mama had to rush to ask for the nurse's assistance. Mama and I prayed.

You know what I did while Mama was downstairs? I kissed Papa twice. I said, *"Papa, we will celebrate Christmas together. Please, don't go! Promise me!"* He could not answer anymore. That was it.

Papa died with me and Mama. Mama said after Papa died, *"Son, we should be thankful the Lord took him already. He was already forgiven from all his sins."* But in my heart I was saying, *"No! I want to be with Papa. He promised me that."* But I cannot do anything anymore. There were times when I just went blank.

I also want to thank everyone. Without you, Papa could not have faced his sickness. *"Thank you Papa, wherever you are, I have always told you, since we started communicating, I always texted you, "Pa, be well. I love you."*

This is all. I hope that you learned something from my sharing. *"Love is love, though painful it is. If you love someone, there's nothing you can do but to return to him."*

TAGALOG

More than 11 years hindi kami nagkasama ng tatay ko, isa lang po ang naramdaman ko. Namiss ko po siya ng sobra. At wala akong magawa kundi magdasal lamang. Lagi ko pong pinagdadasal na sana ok lang siya, na sana… kasi po alam ko po na may sakit siya, na may sakit na po siya noon. Na sana ok lang siya, sana may naga-alaga sa kanya, mga ganun po.

So, napag decidan po namin nila mama na dalawin na si Papa. Kasi nagtext po si mama sabi po niya "anak puntahan na natin si Papa. He is dying. So ako po, nagdasal agad ako. "Lord, sana huwag naman. Gusto ko pang makasama si Papa ng matagal."

So, nung andun na kami sa ospital, nakapagusap kami as a family, heart to heart talk. Nung nailabas namin yung mga matagal na naming itinatago sa puso namin, so ayun sinabi ko kay papa, "Pa, all these years, alam mo Pa, kada pasko isa lang ang hiling ko, na sana magkakasama-sama tayong pamilya. 11 years ko pong hinihiling, hindi ako napagbigyan. Kaya nung sinabi ko kay Papa na… sabi niya sa akin, anak, pina promise ko ngayong pasko magkakasama tayo. So, nag expect ako, kasi yun yung wish ko. Sabi nya, anak lalaban ako para sa atin, para sa pamilya natin. Nung sinabi po sakin ni Papa yun, nag expect ako.

Sobrang miss ko siya. Sa 4 days na nakasama pa namin siya, bale sa akin 5 days, kasi I was there nung mamatay si Papa. Ang mga araw na iyon, nasuklian. Kaya nagpapasalamat ako kay Lord na nabigyan pa kami ng pagkakataon, mga araw na I've been longing for bilang anak, na nakakakuwentuhan mo tungkol sa mga paborito, wrestling, basketball, mga chicks. Nagkuwentuhan kami. Yun yung mga namiss ko, na makapagkuwento ka sa tatay mo ng mga bagay na ganun. Sa limang araw na yun, nagpapaslamat ako kay Lord, nasuklian.

So, nung last day, 6 ng umaga, 6 am, tulog ako. Ginising ako ni mama. At first time ko yatang magising na hindi ako hinahawakan. Isang sigaw lang. Anak gumising ka na! Pagtingin na pagtingin ko, bumangon ako. Namumutla na si Papa. Nakita ko si Mama hirap na hirap. Ramdam ko yung paghihirap ni Papa. Di siya mapakali. Mayat maya iba yung posisyon niya. Ramdam ko yung paghihirap niya. So, ang ginawa namin ni mama simula nung umagang yun, binuksan niya yung laptop, nagplay sya sa youtube ng dasal, nagdasal lang kami ng nagdasal all throughout.

Pero ito yung medyo nakakatawang parte. Kasi mayat maya, may darating na nurse, may ireresetang gamot. Iiwan ako ni mama kailangan niyang bumaba. Ako naman kakapit na ako sa kamay ni Papa. Ipinagdarasal ko, "Lord huwag. Hindi ko kayang ako lang magisa. Dalawang beses na ganun. Pagbaba ni Mama, iniwan ako. Tapos yun na.

Nung moment na yun, si Papa mismo, ramdam na rin niya siguro. Siya mismo inayos nya yung paghiga niya. Diniretso niya yung paa niya, tapos yun na yung last breath niya. Wala kaming magawa ni Mama kundi magdasal. Pero siyempre tumakbo si Mama para sa tulong ng nurse. Nagdasal lang kami ng nagdasal ni Mama.

Alam niyo po kung anong ginawa ko? Habang wala si Mama, ang aking ginawa kiniss ko si Papa dalawang beses. Sabi ko, Pa, magpapasko pa tayo. Huwag! Ipangako mo, sinasabi kong ganun, hindi na sya nakakasagot. Ayun po.

Namatay si Papa nung magkasama kaming dalawa ni Mama. Sabi ni Mama nung namatay na si Papa, anak, we should be thankful kinuha na siya ni Lord. Napatawad na siya sa mga kasalanan niya. Pero sabi ko sa puso ko, hindi gusto kong magpasko kasama si Papa kasi pinangako niya sa akin yun. Pero wala akong magawa. Mayat maya napapatulala ako.

Gusto ko din pong magpasalamat sa inyong lahat. Kung wala po kayo hindi naging ganyan si Papa. Salamat. Papa, kung nasaan ka man, lagi kong sinasabi sa iyo noon, since nagka communication na tayo, lagi kong tinetext sayo, Pa, magpagaling ka ha, I love you.

So, yun lang po. Sana po kapulutan ninyo ng aral. Ang pagibig ay pagibig. Kahit gaano kasakit kung mahal mo yung isang tao babalik at babalik ka sa kanya.

Yun lang po maraming salamat po!

LET US PRAY…

You've molded my son to be a strong, God-fearing, and responsible man, dear God, and I thank you for that. Thank you that despite his pain with his father, you gave both of them the chance to renew their relationship as father and son, the chance to be healed. Anoint him dear Lord, that he may learn from his past and reward him with a happy vocation, be it in marriage or celibacy, and become faithful to that vocation. AMEN.

POINTS TO PONDER…

1. How much time do you spend with your father/mother?
2. Is there something that you've been longing to tell your father/mother and yet you never had the chance to express them?
3. How do you plan to strengthen your relationship with your father/mother?

TALK TO GOD…

____

____

7 LOVE…NOW OR NEVER

"You MUST do this NOW!
Now that they are still alive,
NOW that they can still hear you,
NOW that they can still feel your touch,
NOW that they can still hug you…
Do it NOW before it's too late."
Racquel Helena D. Abagat

*This is Racquel's eulogy during the wake of his Papa. You can watch the video (though incomplete) in these links:
https://www.youtube.com/watch?v=kNWSk2eGOR8
https://www.youtube.com/watch?v=oUEqSmmTx5U

THAT EARLY MORNING when we arrived at the hospital, Papa requested my aunt, *"Sally, can you give us some time? Just us?"* *"Sure, Kuya!"* my aunt answered. And she went down to join my Uncle Tante, at the parking lot.

Only the five of us were in the room. Mama encouraged me and my siblings to speak our minds and express our innermost thoughts, good or bad. Papa started speaking and sincerely asked forgiveness from us, his children and from Mama. After him, Mama said her piece. She told him all her pains and sacrifices but gave emphasis to what is ahead. She begged, *"Let everything in the past end here. From today, let us start anew,"* to which Papa, agreed.

Then it was my turn to speak. I said, *"Papa, alam mo nung una hindi pa ako masyadong convinced. Yung pagpunta namin sa iyo noong March, parang wala pa yun sa akin. Pero noong ma receive ko yung text ni Mama kahapon na sabi niya you're dying, bigla akong nagisip. Sabi ko sa sarili ko, ito na yun. Hindi na ako nakapasok sa klase ko. Nagpaalam na lang ako sa teacher ko at umupo lang ako at nanahimik sa may carabao garden sa campus. Mga 30 minutes akong nakaupo, nagisip at nagdasal. I realized, ito na nga yung time na dapat akong magpatawad."* (**"Papa, you know, at first I was not yet convinced. Our first visit to you in March was nothing to me. But when I received Mama's text message yesterday and she said you were dying, I became quiet. I told myself, this is it! I was not able to attend my class anymore. I asked permission from my teacher. I sat down in one of the benches at the Carabao Garden, for about 30 minutes, reflected and prayed. I realized it was time to forgive."**)

Thank God and I am just so happy that before Papa left us, I was able to sincerely forgive him and spent a few quality days with him.

Those who were here last night, you heard Mama and Ate speak about compassion, love, and forgiveness. Tonight, what I want to share with you are my realizations with everything that happened with me and my family for the past eleven years of separation.

Honestly, if you ask Mama or my siblings about me, they would tell you that I am not that type of person who is expressive of my feelings nor show my real emotions. If I love or like someone, I won't tell you, *"Hey! I love you or I like you."* I will just show you through my actions, either in a good or bad way that I like you or I love you.

I think Papa also knows my personality. Last Thursday morning, when I talked to him I told him that. I knew in my heart, after reflecting at the Carabao Garden, after reading Mama's message that Papa was dying, that I have already forgiven him. But at that very moment when I was talking to Papa, I was able to verbalize my feelings. I said, *"Pa, napatawad na po kita at sana maging ok na tayo."* **(Pa, I have already forgiven you and I hope we will be okay.")** Papa was so happy with what he heard because he knew that I am not that expressive person.

One of my greatest realizations was: we must learn to express our love, affection and forgiveness to someone because doing so means making people happy and liberating us from the negative feeling of un-forgiveness and selfishness. I felt that liberation when I told Papa that I have already forgiven him. It really pays to express and verbalize and not suppress these positive feelings of love and forgiveness.

I am also very happy that Papa's death has brought me and my siblings a chance to meet our relatives and Papa's friends. I have been talking with many of you and there is one thing that I have repeatedly heard, *"proud na proud ang Papa mo sa inyo. Lagi niya kayong kinukuwento."* **("Your Papa is very proud of you. He always tells stories about you.")** Somebody also said, *"may binigay siya sa aking link panoorin daw kita dun sa Opposing Views."* **("He gave me a link he said I should watch you at Opposing Views.")** It made me feel so proud that even if we lived separately for that long, he has remained proud of us and honored to tell people that, *"Mga anak ko yan! Asawa ko yan!"* **("They are my children! She is my wife.")**

What was my realization? My realization was that Papa still loved and cared for us and he remained to be proud of us. Most especially, he was proud of me. I know for a fact that Papa has that *"pride"* used many times in a wrong way. But this time Papa used that *"pride"* in telling people that regardless of his absence, we've continuously worked hard all throughout our lives to prove something. The only thing painful was that he was never there physically to witness my accomplishments. And he would not even be there to witness my greatest achievement which is my university graduation. He was not able to wait for this big day anymore. But it's okay because I know he is now resting with God. I know he has been suffering for so long.

Lastly, I realized the importance of family and the people around who have loved and cared for me, whom I have failed to reciprocally show the same love, care and attention. I have to admit that there are instances in my life when I wanted to say ***"I love you"*** to the people I love. Or even express my gratitude by saying ***"thank you"*** but I failed. I am not a totally rude person who never appreciates the love and care that people around are showering me. I just did not get to learn to express them positively.

And so, I would like to take this opportunity to share this particular struggle I have been through since I was a kid. There may be people here who have the same struggle as mine. I am encouraging you right now. I want you to talk to the person beside you or to whoever you love. Tell them you love them and that you are grateful for their love. Say sorry for all your shortcomings and mistakes. They deserve to be acknowledged, they need to know how you feel, they need to listen to what you want to say.

You MUST do this NOW! Now that they are still alive, NOW that they can still hear you, NOW that they can still feel your touch, NOW that they can still hug you. Do it NOW before it's too late.

My gratitude goes to God, who generously gave me five days to be with Papa. He is such a compassionate God that He allowed me to be healed from this paralysis of inability to express my feelings in a positive way. He has totally healed me from my ungratefulness to people. This experience of Papa's death has brought me a new life- a life of gratitude, love, and forgiveness.

Papa, I may not have expressed this as often as I wanted when you were still alive but please know that I love you so much. I want you to know that at this moment, I have forgiven you. The past can never be undone, but as you said, *"let's move on."*

This is all. Thank you to all who have come to mourn with us. I am sure Papa loves all of you.

LET US PRAY...

Loving God, you performed another healing miracle in my daughter's life. Thank you for making her realize that loving, forgiving, and gratitude liberate her from her inability to appreciate and count her blessings. May she be able to sustain the transformation that she has started with your loving guidance. AMEN.

POINTS TO PONDER...

1. Have your dad/mom been proud of you? How do you feel about it?

2. Are you appreciative or affirmative of the love and recognition given to you by others?

3. What is holding you back from express your feelings towards others?

TALK TO GOD...

____

____

____

____

____

8 5000 PESOS IS PRICELESS

"A sacrifice to be real must cost,
must hurt, must empty ourselves…
If I love until it hurts, then there is no hurt,
but only more love."
Mother Theresa

**AFTER THAT HEART TO HEART family talk, I
and my children felt tired and sleepy so we took a nap.
Renz slept with her Papa on the same bed, Rocev and
Reinier slept on the bench, and Kelly slept sitting down.
Though I was tired, I could not sleep. I was just staring at
all of them while they were all asleep. I never imagined
that this will happen. What I was seeing at that moment
was unthinkable.**

At around 10:30 in the morning, Rod started to complain. He said it was very hot and requested Reinier to increase the aircon temperature. He did. But he still complained. My son and I took turns in manually fanning him. He held me by the waist and he repeatedly whispered, *"Ma, please don't leave me."* I assured him we will not leave him.

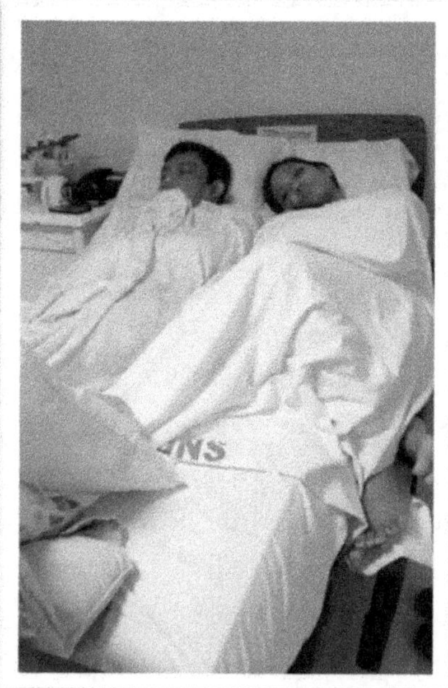

Renz taking a nap with her Papa after that heart to heart talk with him.

After a while he complained again. This time he said he felt cold. He asked my son to lower down the aircon temperature and stop fanning him. We did. Then he had difficulty breathing. He was gasping. I felt his pain but what could I do? I kept praying. While praying I kept on looking at each of my children, telling them to pray as well. I whispered, *"Pa, kaya mo yan, lumaban ka. Andito lang kami. Hindi kami aalis."* **(Pa, you can do it. We are just here. We will not leave you.)** He hugged me tightly. He did not want to let go of my arms wrapped around his head.

Then the nurses and doctors came. They checked his blood sugar and blood pressure. Everything dropped. He was injected emergency medicines to normalize his blood sugar and another medicine for his blood pressure. Some of his relatives and friends were there. We were all speechless. But I felt that we were thinking of the same thing. *"Is this his time?"* Did he just wait for us so we can talk?

I heard the doctor telling my mother-in-law that Rod needed an emergency dialysis. The doctor explained that the water content of his body increased that's why he was swelling. My mother-in-law approached me and asked for my opinion. I said if I were to decide, I would go for the dialysis but we should ask the patient. So, Mommy asked Rod and he said, *"Oo, Mommy. Gusto ko nang magpa-dialysis. Ayaw ko pang mamatay. Nangako ako sa mga anak ko na magsasama sama pa kami"* **(Yes, Mommy. I want to undergo dialysis. I don't want to die yet. I promised my children we will be together.)**

So, with that, I felt relieved. He slowly regained his breath but he kept on whispering, *"Ma, please don't leave me."* I assured him again that we won't leave him. I noticed the doctor and the nurses coming to our room around three times to ask whether we have made the deposit at the cashier for the dialysis. Every time they ask the question, my mother-in-law answered, *"Opo!"* **(Yes!)** So, I thought everything was ready.

After a while, Renz approached and whispered, *"Ma, tinatanong ni Mommy kung may pera ka daw kasi kailangan ng pang deposit sa hospital. Sabi ko naman malamang wala kasi biglaan ang uwi mo."* **(Ma, Mommy is asking if you have money because they need money to be deposited to the hospital. I told her maybe you don't have because you had to rush home.)** I answered, *"Paano yan? Wala talaga kasi yung ibinili kong ticket ay nakisuyo lang ako sa credit card ng kaibigan ko. Ikaw anak baka may natitira ka pang pera. Ipahiram mo muna."* **(How's that? I really don't have money because I had to borrow my friend's credit card to be able to buy a ticket. Maybe you still have some money left. Lend it.)** My daughter was hesitant because that was her last money from the first teaching job that she had. I convinced her, *"Sige na anak, ipahiram mo na. Ako na lang ang magsasauli sa iyo pag nagkapera ako."* **Come on baby, lend it. I will return it to you when I have extra money.)**

She went to the ATM at the ground floor of the hospital and withdrew her last money of 5,000 pesos. She gave the money to my mother-in-law and both went to the billing department of the hospital. Renz begged the staff to allow her Papa to have his dialysis with that amount and the remaining 10,000 pesos will be given a little later. That time my sister-in-law, Marisa, was also busy looking for money to pay the incurred hospital bills, and the additional money needed for the dialysis. Being an emergency case the staff finally gave in to my daughter's request.

At around 1:00 in the afternoon, Rod went through dialysis.

While he was at the operating room, we looked for the cheapest and nearest hotel where we could sleep and rest. The hospital administration immediately gave our room to another patient when Rod was brought to the operating room so we had no place to stay.

He was brought to the ICU at around 5:30 in the afternoon. The very sight of him with all the tubes connected to his body was also painful for me. *Why did all these have to happen?* I asked the security guard if I can bring all my four children inside so that they can see their Papa. He kindly allowed us. So, I brought the four kids inside.

They looked at their Papa with compassion. I also could feel their pain to see their father in that condition.

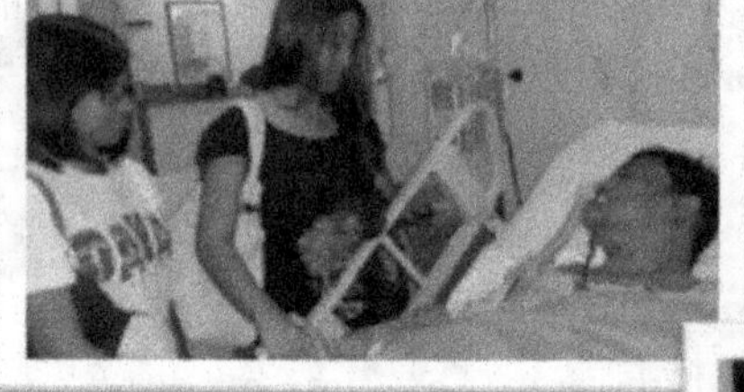

The children visited Rod at the ICU immediately after his dialysis.

At around 6:30 in the evening, I thought of inviting a priest to give him the Sacrament of the Anointing of the Sick. I requested my brother to drive us to the College of the Holy

Spirit Tarlac. I know some of the Sisters there so perhaps they can refer us to a priest. Unfortunately, the school was closed already and the students who were still inside informed us that we should go to Tanedo because the sisters moved their convent there.

I persisted. We went to the church. The sacristan or perhaps the one in charge of the church told us that all priests are in Baguio for a retreat. But still, I did not give up. A young guy, perhaps a staff of the parish office, heard us and he approached us. He said, *"May kilala po akong mga pari sa Don Bosco. Sila po ay hindi kasama sa Baguio. Samahan ko na po kayo."* ***(I know some priests at Don Bosco. They are not in Baguio now. I will bring you there.)*** *"Thank God!"* I muttered. I immediately told him to get in the car. So, we all went together to Don Bosco. He talked to the security guard. He was told that the Principal, a priest, was there. The guard contacted the priest's residence to check if the priest was available. After a while, we were told to wait.

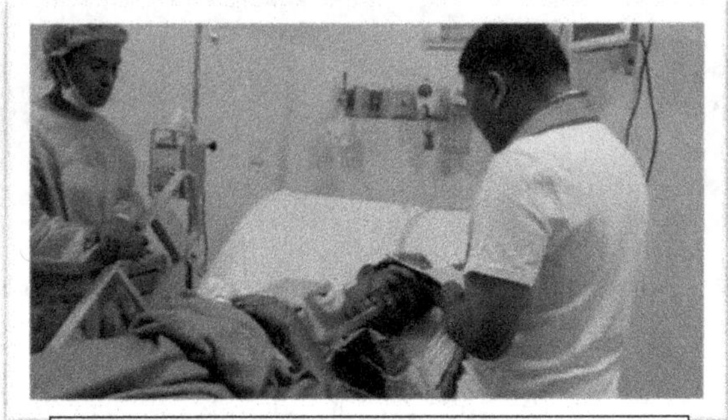

Rod receives the Sacrament of the Anointing of the Sick from Fr. Abel after his dialysis.

Then the priest came. He is Fr. Abel. He gladly came with us to the hospital. Rod received the Sacrament at around 8:00 in the evening.

We thanked Fr. Abel after that and he, together with the guy, were brought back to Don Bosco by my brother.

I firmly believed that by the grace, mercy, and compassion of God, he was given spiritual and physical strength. I was grateful for the people God used as instruments for us to be able to invite a priest to give him the Sacrament. I and my children were very grateful to my very patient and supportive brother, Kuya Tante, who was with us all throughout.

The next day, he looked a lot better. AMEN! He was regaining his strength although the tubes were still connected to him. I and my children took turns in taking care of him at the ICU. I and the two boys were on duty during the evening time to around 3:00 or 4:00 in the morning. My brother drove the two girls at around that time to the hospital, and brought me and the boys to the hotel to take a nap and rest until around 8:00 or 9:00 in the morning.

During those times, the children had intimate moments with their Papa. They told me later that they shared a lot of happy memories and stories together. They treasured those moments.

I had my intimate moments with him, too at the ICU especially the two mornings when the children were still asleep at the hotel. We remembered the happy memories of our marriage-- when the kids were growing up. We planned to spend Christmas 2014 as a family in Ilocos.

Although there were awkward moments, they were funny at the same time, like when we were thinking of a title just in case our love story gets featured at Maalaala Mo Kaya -MMK (a television drama about true-to-life stories), or when the nurse asked me if he was wearing dentures but I couldn't answer because I have totally forgotten, or when the doctor asked his address and I didn't even know, or when they asked me if he was a PhilHealth member and I answered that I will ask my mother-in-law. Maybe the nurses and the doctors were all wondering.

On his third day at the ICU he was transferred to a regular room. He looked perfectly all right. He looked skinnier because the water was removed from his body. He ate regular meals. He showed much progress. On Sunday, he entertained many visitors by his stories. He

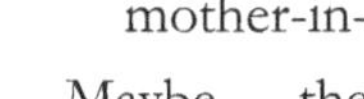

Time spent with Rod at the ICU after his dialysis.

was the usual him, cracking jokes to everyone. I saw him many times watching his children play and share jokes. I could see his happiness. He repeatedly said, *"Ma, salamat at inalagaan mo ng maayos ang mga bata."* **(Ma, thank you for taking good care of the children.)** I told him, *"Hindi ba yan naman ang pangako sa iyo? Na hindi ko sila pababayaan?"* **(Is that not my promise to you? That I will take good care of them?)**

But death was inevitable. He joined the Creator the morning of November 17, 2014.

We were on our way back to Laguna after the cremation when Renz suddenly said, *"Ma, ngayon ko lang na realize. Yun palang 5,000 pesos ko yun ang nakapagdugtong ng buhay ni Papa ng limang araw."* **(Ma, I only realized now. My 5,000 pesos extended Papa's life for five days.)**

I was stunned with that realization of my daughter. I said, *"Tama anak. Biruin mo, kung hindi dahil sa inambag mong kahuli-hulihang pera mo ay hindi na natin nakasama ng limang araw ang Papa mo?"* **(You're right! Imagine, if you did not share your last money, we could not have spent five days with your Papa?)**

"Oo nga, Ma," **(Yes, Mama!)** she agreed. Even my aunts and sister-in-law who were with us agreed and praised Renz for that good act. So, I jokingly said, *"So, hindi ko na babayaran sayo yun ha?"* **(So, I will not pay you anymore?)** She said, *"Sige huwag na. Contribution ko na yun. Kaso hindi na yun alam ni Papa."* **(It's all right. Never mind. That is already my**

*contribution. **But the thing is Papa does not know it anymore.**)* I said, *"Anak alam niya yun. Hindi naman kailangang sabihin para malaman niya. At alam ng Diyos yun."* **(Baby, he knows that. There is no need to tell him or for him to know. God knows).** *"Oo nga,"* **(Ah, yes!)** she agreed. And we all laughed.

While we were on our way, her realization kept reverberating in my mind. *"Yun palang 5,000 pesos ko ang nakapagpadugtong ng buhay ni Papa ng limang araw….."* **(My 5,000 pesos extended Papa's life for five days….)**

I still could not believe, but everything happened in just five days… just five days… all the years gone were regained in just five days… My daughter had to sacrifice that very little resource, the very last she had, for the love of her Papa. It was indeed priceless!

LET US PRAY...

Compassionate God, thank you for teaching us, especially my daughter, the real meaning of selfless love and sacrifice. Thank you also for giving us the chance to spend five priceless and memorable days together as a family for forgiveness and healing to take place. I pray that my children may continue to share, be generous, and give without counting the cost, to sacrifice until it hurts and love eternally. This I pray, Amen!

POINTS TO PONDER...

    1.   What sacrifices do you often do for others?

2. What is the most painful sacrifice that you have ever made for someone you love?

3. How do you feel after sharing something, or offering some help, or sacrificing for someone?

TALK TO GOD...

____

____

____

____

____

____

9 A FATHER'S LOVE IS IRREPLACEABLE

"Fathers, do not provoke your children to anger,
But bring them up in the discipline
and instruction of the Lord."
Ephesians 6:4

ONE MORNING WHILE HAVING BREAKFAST, my youngest son, Rocev Miguel who was only ten years old then said, *"Ma, gusto ko pong magkaroon ng Papa."* *(Mom I want to have a father.)* **I was taken aback by what he said.** *"Naiinggit po ako sa mga kaklase ko. Meron silang family,"* *(I envy my classmates. They have a family.)* **Afterwards, he started to cry.**

This conversation melted my heart. I started sobbing, myself. I hugged him tightly while saying, *"Sige anak. Ipagdasal natin yan. Kung will ni God, then mangyayari. Wag ka ng umiyak,"* **(OK baby, let's start praying for that. If it's God's will, then it**

will happen. Stop crying, ok?) and embraced him even tighter. We cried together while in each other's arms, hoping and praying for God's will.

I perfectly understand the emptiness deep inside him that only a real father could give. I know he misses a father whom he can play with, whom he can share stories with, and whom he can learn from. I know the pain he felt every time I allowed him to visit his friend to play and see his friend's father in the house. It was heart breaking but the situation then was just too difficult to explain to him.

I know God has blessed me with a wonderful family. My children lived with my very loving father for more than a year before he died. During that time that they were with him, they felt and experienced the unconditional love of a real father. My brothers and brothers-in-law became more than fathers to them, especially my eldest sister's husband, Kuya Martin. The love and concern they have shown my children were incomparable. But perhaps the love of a "real" father is really different.

We made attempts to visit my husband but we were not yet ready. I asked my children to write him instead and tell him some updates about their studies, what they were busy with, at the same time greet him because he was soon celebrating his birthday. This is what Rocev Miguel wrote:

Happy Birthday nga po pala. Musta ka naman po? Ok ka lang ba jan? Natatandaan mo po ba ako? Ako yung bunso niyo. Si Rocev. Masaya po ba kayo na wala kami sa inyo? Hehe...

Happy birthday! How are you? Are you okay? Do you still remember me? I am Rocev. Are you happy that we are not with you? Hehe!

Masarap po ba yung feeling na lumaki ka ng walang naggagabay na ama sa iyo? Diba po hindi? Pero kinaya ko kasi meron akong nanay na tumatayo ko ring tatay sa araw-araw kong pangangailangan. Salamat po dahil kahit papano ay hindi niyo po kami naisipang hanapin at kausapin. Kahit papano po. Meron pa rin akong unting natitirang pagmamahal sa inyo.

Does it feel good to grow up without a father guiding you? It isn't, right? But I did it because I have a mother who is at the same time my father who attends to my everyday needs. Thank you that you did not look for us or talk to us anymore. Despite everything, I still love you.

Ang iyong bunso, **(Your youngest child)**
Rocev

While reading this, I couldn't help but cry my heart out. I didn't expect him to be this expressive about his feelings. But this is how he feels. Feelings are feelings! They cannot be wrong at all and I respect him. I did not tell him to revise or change the letter. I did not also attempt to edit it. I sent the letter to my husband. He should listen and feel the message.

I know it was not healthy for him to be harboring this kind of sentiments towards his father but it was a product of his experiences with him. Growing up without the presence of a real father, though he was just kilometers away, was not at all easy. I faithfully prayed for healing, emotional healing for my children, especially for Rocev Miguel who was only two to three years old when my husband and I separated. He was too young that he cannot even remember the face of his father, except when he sees him in pictures.

When we decided to finally meet my husband and when we were about to reach my mother-in-law's house, he said *"Ma, natatakot po ako."* **(Ma, I'm scared.)** I held his hand and confidently I assured him, *"Wag kang matakot anak. Basta kasama niyo ako walang mangyayaring masama."* **(Don't be scared, son. As long as you are with me, nothing wrong will happen.)** When my husband had the chance to talk to him, he said, *"Anak, tanggalin mo na yang galit sa puso mo ha. Sorry, anak."* **(Son, remove the anger in your heart. Sorry, son.)**

Five days before my husband died, we had the chance to talk and express our deep-seated sentiments buried in our hearts for eleven years. My eldest daughter started. Not long after she started speaking, Rocev Miguel started to sob. He was the first one to cry. I could feel the pain but I knew in my heart that my son's tears were tears of joy, tears of healing, catharsis from a lonely and traumatic childhood spent without a father. It was a cry of liberation from pain. After that, he spent a few days to take care of his father, they shared unforgettable memories of each other's past, talked about wrestling, basketball, music, and others.

Upon Rod's death, every 17th of the month was declared by my children as **"Pasta Day"** to commemorate his demise. Spaghetti is Rod's (and my two sons) favorite food. We make sure that we eat pasta/spaghetti on this date, even by ourselves because we live far from each other.

On July 17, 2015, while we were feasting on instant pasta and toast bread (spaghetti for Rocev Miguel and carbonara for me, and since we were on a tight budget, we settled for the instant pasta), he blurted, *"Mama ang hirap pala,"* **(Mama, I realize it's difficult.)** He was teary eyed. I asked, *"Mahirap ang alin."***(Which one is difficult?)** He shrugged his shoulders and answered, *"Wala lang."***(Nothing.)**

There, I began to feel my tears cloud my eyes but I had to control it because I didn't want Rocev to see me cry. I encouraged him to tell me honestly what was disturbing him. Finally, he said he missed his friends in the Philippines. Then he added, *"ang hirap Mama kasi nangako ako kay Papa na aalagaan kita at hindi kita iiwan. Nangako ako sa kanya na hindi ako magiging katulad niya."* **(Mama it's so difficult because I promised Papa that I will not leave you. I promised him that I will not be like him.)** I couldn't hide my tears any longer. I was totally speechless. I just hugged him tightly and thanked him. So sweet of him.

Then I told him I perfectly understand his situation. I know it was difficult for him to come to Korea and leave his friends behind, transferring to another school for the $\underline{n}$th time (he's into his 7th school since he started nursery), and still having to wait for the final decision as to where his next school would be. Everything was uncertain for him but I reminded him that whatever happens, it's going to be God's will. I know how he felt but since he promised his Papa that he will take care of me, he decided to go with me, though it was a big sacrifice on his part. I encouraged him to study hard because that will make his father happier. He smiled and we both stopped crying.

His faithfulness to his promise, despite giving up his own happiness, is a sign of love, total healing, and forgiveness to his father. My son may not have experienced the love of a real father, but his grandfather and uncles have loved him unconditionally as their own son. My heartfelt thanks goes to them for without them, Rocev could not have grown to be a good boy.

Most of all, his Father in heaven have brought him up to be a good son, and to be a good, responsible father in the future. It's God who took away the anger in him, and replaced it with love. What a blessing!!!!

So, to all the fathers in the world, remember that your love is definitely irreplaceable in your children's hearts. Do not provoke them to anger, instead, bring them up in the discipline and instruction of the Lord.

LET US PRAY...

Heavenly Father, the father of all fathers, thank you for allowing my son to experience the love of a real father. Though brief, he felt a father's embrace, a father's presence, and a father's touch. In so short a time, you taught him to forgive, you healed him, and you made him a responsible young man. May you guide him as he matures to be the real man you want him to become. This I pray. AMEN!

POINTS TO PONDER...

1. Do you have any resentments or bad feeling towards your own father? What is it?
2. What do you plan to do with this feeling?
3. How do you think can you patch up your relationship with him?

TALK TO GOD...

10 MOVE ON

"Brothers, I do not consider that I have made it my own.
But one thing I do: forgetting what lies behind
and straining forward to what lies ahead…"
Philippians 3:13

WHILE I WAS TAKING CARE of my husband in the hospital, he entrusted his two phones with me for safekeeping. Though it had passwords, he eventually revealed this to me and it was unexpected that he had been using a password that we have commonly used when we were still living together.

So, in those few days we were with him, I had access to his phones especially when he was asleep because some messages would come and I happen to accidentally read some of them.

One girl's message read: *"Dadalawin na lang kita uli sa susunod ha. Anong gusto mong kainin? Ipagluluto kita. Dadalhan kita ng pagkain sa susunod na dalaw ko. Baka bukas o sa susunod na araw puntahan kita uli."* ***(I will visit you again next time. What do you want to eat? I will cook for you. I will bring some food next time I visit you. Maybe tomorrow or the next day, I will see you again.)*** Of course there were replies from my husband. Honestly, that message was nothing to me. I ignored it until I totally forgot about it.

Then another girl sent this message: *"Gustong gusto kitang makita. Nagpunta ako sa ospital kanina kaya lang nakita ko si Mommy sa baba. Sabi niya huwag na daw akong tumuloy kasi andyan daw ang pamilya mo at ang asawa mo ang naga-alaga sa iyo."* ***(I really wanted to see you. I went to the hospital a while ago but I met Mommy downstairs. She said I'd better not come because your family is there and your wife is the one taking care of you.)*** Again, of course there were responses from my husband. Honestly, this message hit me. Not only because I was jealous but also by the very thought of two things: One, until now, Rod hasn't changed, and two, my mother-in-law knew all the while. Again…

On his second day at the ICU (Intensive Care Unit), a girl came. It was my first time to see her. I was my natural ME, kind and nice. I offered her a chair but she said it's okay to remain standing. So, I did not insist. It was unusual because normally I am introduced by my husband to anyone who visits him that I do not know. When she left, I asked him, *"Sino siya?"* ***(Who is***

she?) He said, *"Ah siya si blah blah blah…. "* **(Ah she is blah blah blah….)** I did not even bother to remember her name because I was not that interested.

At around 12:30 in the afternoon, the guard knocked at the door. He said somebody wanted to visit but because Renz and I were inside, she cannot enter as only two people were allowed inside the ICU. So, I went out to meet that somebody and found out that it was the same girl who visited that morning. She was holding something in a plastic container. I was about to get it from her but she insisted on getting inside. The guard cannot do anything but let her come in.

When she entered the room, she immediately handed over the plastic container to my husband. They were talking in their dialect but I perfectly understood what they were talking about. She said she made some dish for him. When I heard that, the text message I read previously flashe back to my mind. Aha! So this is the girl who sent the message.

I remained calm. I prepared his lunch and fed him. I gave him the dish the girl prepared. But there were lots of leftover. So, that night, I told Mommy to bring home the leftover. She asked me who gave it and I answered it came from a girl named Joan (not her real name), while observing mommy's reaction. She justified, *"Ah kaibigan namin siya. Minsan ipinagluluto niya kami, Nakkong."* **(Ah she is our friend. Sometimes she cooks for us, Nakkong--an endearing name for a son or daughter.)** I just said, *"Ah okay Mommy!"* No questions asked. Her answer said it all.

Sunday night, my three children and my brother had to leave for Los Banos. Before they left, Renz, told him, *"Papa, ikaw ha mag behave ka! Huwag mong bibigyan ng sakit ng ulo si Mama. Hirap na hirap na siya. Itetext kita minu-minuto, oras-oras."* **(Papa, you must behave. Don't give Mama a headache. She is in much difficulty already. I will text you every minute and every hour.)** I butted in, *"Syempre naman lagi kang itetext ni Papa mo. Ang dami kaya niyang katext."* **(Of course your Papa will always text you. He has many textmates.)** My husband smiled. I could read what was going in his mind. For sure, he will surely change his password.

True enough! At dawn, around 3:30 in the morning, Reinier, woke me up to be with my husband because he was already sleepy. I checked his phone again. The password has been changed. Well, what he didn't realize was I already saved the phone numbers in my phone.

At around 10:00 in the morning when my husband started to feel uneasy and had difficulty breathing, I started to pray. In my prayer, something popped up in my head. *"These girls deserve to know that he is dying. Call them!"*

Despite the tension, rush and the panic inside the room, I managed to send a text message to the two girls. I said, *"Mamamatay na siya. Kung gusto niyo pa siyang makita at* *makausap, pumunta na kayo ngayon habang makakausap niyo pa. Asawa niya ito. Huwag kayong matakot hindi ako galit." (**He is dying. If you still want to see him and talk to him, come now while you can still talk to him. This is his wife. Don't be scared. I'm not angry.**)*

One of the girls sent back a message. She said, *"Talaga po? Huwag naman po kayong magsalita ng ganyan." (**Really? Please don't say like that.**)* I answered, *"hindi ako nagbibiro. Totoo ang sinasabi ko." (**I'm not joking. What I'm saying is true.**)* Then she texted back again, *"Gusto ko sanang pumunta kaso nasa Manila na ako. Dito kasi ang trabaho ko." (**I wanted to come but I'm already in Manila. I work here.**)* I replied, *"E di tawagan mo siya." (**Then call him.**)* Her funny answer was, *"Hindi po ako makatawag, wala po akong load." (I cannot call I don't have a load.)* I replied, *"Ano ba gamit mo? Globe o Smart?" (**What do you use, Globe or Smart?**)*

Honestly, I wanted to share a load so she can call Rod but even before I could have received her answer whether she was using Smart or Globe, she already called. That time I was at the pharmacy because the doctor asked me to buy some emergency medicines to pump up Rod's blood pressure. She was crying on the phone. I said, *"nasa parmasiya ako tumawag ka na lang sa phone niya." (**I am at the pharmacy. Call his phone.**)* After buying the medicine, I immediately went up. While I was at the door, Rod's phone was ringing. I told my son to give the phone to his Papa. That time he was already in sheer pain and his hands were shaking that he cannot hold his phone anymore. I asked my son to hold it for him. In Capangpangan, he said, *"Pota na ka maus. Malilyo ko."* ***(Call later. I'm dizzy.)*** He hanged the phone.

A few minutes later, he died. I texted the girl, *"Wala na siya."* ***(He's gone.)*** She called immediately. Again she was crying on the phone. In a firm, loud, and fierce voice I said, *"Mamaya ka na tumawag at busy pa kami dito. Pero andito ang kapatid nya at Mommy. Gusto mo ba silang makausap?"* ***(Call later because we are all busy here. But his brother and Mommy are here. Would you like to talk to them?)*** She said, *"Opo!"* ***(Yes!)***

I handed the phone to Mommy, *"Mommy, may gusto pong kumausap sa inyo."* ***(Mommy, somebody wants to talk to you.)*** *"Sino yan Nakkong?"* ***(Who is that Nakkong?)*** she asked. *"Sheila (not her real name) daw po ang pangalan,"* (Her name is *Sheila.)* I replied. She took the phone and shouted in Capangpangan *"Nakputa ka ut mamaus ka pa?"* ***(F—- why do you have to call?)*** I took the phone from her, *"Mommy, hindi niyo na po dapat ginawa yun. Alam ko naman na."* ***(Mommy, you should not have done that. I know it anyway.)*** She kept quiet.

While Rod was being dressed up at the funeral parlor, I was sitting beside my son and Mommy. A girl walked towards us but I did not recognize her. She stood right in front of me for a few seconds, but I just stared at her because I cannot recall where and when I saw her. I was stunned and I could not utter a single word. She walked away and went in the direction where Rod's brother, Mommy, and my sister-in-law were standing.

My son called my attention, *"Mama, ikaw ha naging bitch ka."* **(Mama, you acted like a bitch.)** I asked, *"why?"* Reinier said, *"inaabot niya yung kamay niya tapos hindi mo pinansin."* **(she was extending her hand but you ignored her.)** I answered, *"Naku anak, sorry. Hindi ko alam. Iniisip ko kasi kung saan ko siya nakita. Hindi ko siya makilala."* **(Sorry, son. I didn't know. I was trying to recall where I saw her. I didn't recognize her.)**

Then I asked the girl beside me, *"Sino na nga po yun?"* **(who is she?)** She replied, *"Si Joan po."* **(She is Joan)** My reaction was, *"Ah… si Joan… in person!"* **(Ah… so she's Joan…in person!)**

She defensively replied, *"Narinig ko nga po pero di ko alam kung totoo."* **(I heard about it but I don't know if it's true.)** I answered back, *"Hindi naman po mahalaga kung totoo o hindi. Actually, tinext ko siya kanina pang umaga."* **(It's not important whether it's true or not. Actually, I texted her this morning.)** She was surprised, *"talaga po?"* **(Really?)** I just nodded.

On December 17, 2014, we went to Tarlac to commemorate Rod's 40th death-day, or 40 days as it is commonly called. My mother-in-law introduced me to another girl, who apparently, claimed that Rod owed her $2,000 USD and she wanted me to pay for it. In one part of our conversation I directly asked her, *"Sorry kung tatanungin ko ito sa iyo. Kasi ginawa ko din ito sa ibang mga nakarelasyon nya. Nagkaroon ba kayo ng relasyon ni Rod?"* **(Sorry if I ask you this question. I also did this to others whom he had relationships with. Did you and Rod also have a relationship?)** Her eyes started to roll as if trying to look for a safe answer. After a few seconds she answered, *"Hmmmm sabihin na po nating Kuya ganun, parang Kuya lang."* **(Hmmm… let's say big brother, just like a big brother.)**

Without further interrogation I said, *"Salamat! Salamat kasi kahit papano may mga pangangailangan siguro si Rod na natugunan ninyo during our absence sa buhay niya. Alam kong hindi rin naging madali para sa inyo. Kaya gusto kitang pasalamatan. Salamat!"* **(Thank you! Thank you because most probably Rod had needs that you and the other girls have provided during our absence in his life. I know it was not also easy for you. That's why I want to thank you. Thank you!)**

Move on! We all had to move on with our lives because in one way or the other they have also been victims. After everything that has happened, I felt I had to thank them too. I believe that thanking them will make it easier for all of us to start anew. In my mind, all I needed was to forget what was behind and push forward to what lies ahead.

LET US PRAY...

You have nurtured in me the heart to understand, to see the goodness in people no matter how bad they would seem. This is such a wonderful gift from you, Oh God. Through this I can understand others more and easier for me to forgive. May you continue to nourish this in me, dear Lord, for this is what I need to be able to reach out to more people who are broken and craving to be whole again. AMEN.

POINTS TO PONDER...

1. Do you hold back grudges and hurts? How long?
2. What do you do to release these grudges? Do you confront? Dialogue? Write?
3. Have you any effort to know and understand why people act the way they do?

TALK TO GOD...

____

____

____

____

____

11 GOD IS STRONGEST AT YOUR WEAKEST

"My grace is sufficient for you
For my strength is made perfect in weakness."
2 Corinthians 12:9

THE KIDS ASKED, "Mama, bakit ganun si Papa? Laging nakasigaw at laging nagmumura?" (Why is Papa like that? He is always shouting and saying bad words?) I've always defended him saying, "Anak, intindihin niyo na lang si Papa. May sakit kasi kaya laging mainit ang ulo. Gusto lang niya kayong maging mabait." (Children, please understand Papa. He is sick that's why he is always hot-tempered. He just wants you to be good kids). Everything they did, like using the computer, watching television, playing or eating something from the refrigerator always require their Papa's permission. On

Saturdays, the children would ask, "Mama, may pasok si Papa?" (Mama, is Papa going to work?) And when I answered yes, they'd say "Yehey!" Once they hear the gate opening, they look through the window and they begin to rejoice. It was a very unhealthy atmosphere.

At about the end of March 2003, I talked to my three children and I opened up what I felt for their Papa. I said I cannot bear the sufferings anymore. The kids started recounting their Papa's dreadful attitude every time he gets angry.

Renz, who was only eleven said, *"Mama, bakit ganun si papa? Laging nakasigaw tapos nagsasabi ng hayop kayo, mga animal kayo,….(****Mama, why is Papa like that? He always shouts and says you're animals..)*** *And all those bad words?"*

Racquel, who was only eight years old added *"Oo nga mama pero ako wala akong maalala na pinalo ako ni Papa."* **(Yes, Mama but I don't remember Papa spanking me).**

And Reinier, who was only six years old recalled, *"Ako mama di ba binugbog na ako ni Papa noong pinaglaruan ko yung gamot ni Rocev?"* **(In my case Mama, isn't it Papa hit me when I played with Rocev's medicine?)**

The two children nodded. And they remembered, *"Tapos puro pasa ka sa katawan? Tapos puro bawal, bawal manood ng TV, bawal lumabas, bawal maglaro"* **(And you had bruises all over your body? Then everything is not allowed. We are not** *allowed to watch TV, we are not allowed to go out, we are not allowed to play).*

"Anak, magdesisyon tayo. Iiwanan na ba natin si Papa?" **(Children, let's decide. Are we going to leave Papa?)** I solicited for their opinions.

They unanimously answered *"Mama, pagbigyan pa natin si Papa. Susulatan namin siya. Anyway anniversary niyo naman sa April 6."* **(Mama, let's give Papa another chance. We will write him. Anyway it's going to be your anniversary on April 6.)**

Whoa! Though unexpected for they, too, were subject to their Papa's harshness, that was the sweetest answer I got from these children. Thank God for giving me these angels. Though they were still very young, they were firm in their decision to give their Papa another chance. So, the three of them wrote some simple notes telling him how much they love him and put it in his locker. When he read the letters, he accused me of instructing them on what to write.

One time he was asked to emcee a program in school but since he was absent, the verbal invitation was sent through me. When I informed him, he accused me of recommending him. He asked me to write a script but since I was busy tending the children I failed to write one for him.

That night, he was so upset and texted me, *"Hindi mo ako mahal, wala akong silbi sa iyo, maglalaslas na lang ako."* **(You don't** *love me. I'm useless. I'll just hurt myself).* I immediately went down and checked on him. I saw him hurting himself with a kitchen knife. I attempted to go near him but he threatened that he would stab me so I kept my distance from him. In my desperation to put an end to his foolishness, I knelt before him trembling, begging him to stop.

I went back to our room and wrote the script. When I finished I brought it to him. After reading the script, he tore it off. I cannot really understand what he was up to. He was again shouting. I tried to pacify him for fear that the children and the whole neighborhood will hear him.

He asked me to write it again. The problem was that I was not able to save the document in my computer so I had to pick up the torn pieces of paper and put it together. I re-typed the whole thing.

But before I was done, he came to the room holding a knife. His eyes were fierce and trembling in anger then he said *"Sino? Sino sa mga anak mo ang gusto mong unahin ko?"* **(Who among your kids would you like me to kill first?)**

When I heard this, I immediately embraced him. At that point, I did not care if he will thrust the knife and kill me. All I wanted was to save my four children, who at that time were all sleeping. They had no idea of what was happening. I felt my world stopped for a few seconds.

After that, I don't exactly know what had happened but he suddenly became so weak. He fell on the bed, falling asleep with the knife in his hands. Slowly, I took the knife from him.

The next day, he woke up and prepared himself for school, ready to emcee the program as if nothing has happened the night before.

February 13, 2003, I went to Mindoro to arrange the Outreach Program of the Graduate School. He did allow me to go but he started texting me negative things like *"Siguro kasama mo lalake mo ano? Ano ginagawa ninyo? Nag e-enjoy ka ba?"* **(Maybe you are with your boyfriend, right? What are you doing? Are you enjoying?)** Though peeved, I tried to keep my composure in front of the teachers and the owners of the school. He was calling me the whole night but I did not answer. The next day, he said he was sorry and begged me to go home soonest because he misses me.

At about 11:00 pm of February 14, he invited me to join him at Ate Mel's Restaurant because he was drinking with some of his friends. When I arrived, his mood suddenly changed and he said, *"Gusto mo mag iskandalo ako dito, gusto mo pasuin kita ng sigarilyo? Bakit ayaw mo mapahiya?* **(Do you want me to make a scandal here, do you want me to burn you with my cigarette? Why don't you want to be embarrassed?)** I pretended to be all right in front of everyone.

The next day, I had to go to the office very early because there were thesis defenses scheduled for that day. In the afternoon, Nina invited me to have coffee with Atty. Louie, one of the Graduate School Faculty. Nina knew what I was going through so she recommended I should take a break. I agreed.

While having coffee, Atty. Louie said he knew how it felt to be waiting for the result of the BAR exams. I called my husband and invited him to join us but he was not answering his phone. So, Atty. Louie suggested that maybe he can visit him at home and have some beer. I thought it was a good idea.

On our way home, I received a text message from him saying *"Putang ina mo, lumalandi ka na naman."* **(Fuck you! You're flirting again.)** I told him we were on our way home but he was not satisfied. He texted Nina and said *"Pakisabi kay Emely putangina niya."* **(Please tell Emely fuck.)**

When we arrived home, he was inside our room and when he saw me, he shut the door. So I went up to see him, but he kicked me at my back and punched me both on my left and right arms saying the F word. I never cried, I never complained, I never shouted, I never fought back. I just told him *"Papa, andiyan si Attorney, may sasabihin siya sa iyo."* **(Papa, Attorney is here he wants to tell you something).** After some time, he went down and talked to Atty. Louie but he left instantly. After that, seemingly nothing has happened.

On February 17, 2003, I consulted a doctor at Calamba Medical Center because of the physical pain and bruises all over my body as a result of his recurrent battering. At that point in time I wanted everything documented. The doctor asked me what happened so I told him the real reason. Then he suggested, *"Ma'am I think you need to consult a psychiatrist. We have one right in front of my clinic."*

I acceded to his suggestion. I narrated the whole story from the beginning. After listening to my story, the psychiatrist disclosed, *"Ma'am, based on your story, your husband is suffering from manic depression and needs immediate confinement. He needs to be treated."* I was shocked with what I heard.

"Are you the one preparing his food?" he asked. I nodded. *"If I prescribe some medicines, can you put it in his food?"* he inquired. *"Doctor, I can't. He is paranoid. He suspects that I am putting "vetsin/msg" in his food. If he finds out that I am putting medicine on his food, he will surely kill me,"* I answered. *"Then you have to convince him to seek professional help with you."*

So, in one of our "light moments," I asked him *"Pa, remember one time you told me you felt you were sick and you needed professional help? Would you like to seek professional help with me?"* He answered yes. But after a few seconds he said *"I don't like. I'm not sick."* So I did not pursue the issue for fear that this might lead to another heated argument.

He was extremely depressed during the day as he stays in bed the whole day, but he was utmost active during the night. He was awake the whole night watching TV, listening to music, or sometimes doing the laundry. There were times when he would just burst in anger and text me nasty things at the middle of the night like *"mas mahal mo trabaho mo, di mo ako mahal, bad words like putang-ina mo, hindot ka, pabigat ka sa buhay ko, buwisit ka,…"* **(You love your work more than me, you don't love me, fuck you, you're a burden to me…)** I went to work every day, pretending that everything was okay. But when night time comes, I dreaded going home for fear of what is going to happen again during the night.

Then I realized that everything was eating me up. I could not focus on my work anymore. I had to attend to my children's needs but he competes with them. One time my kids were asking me for something and he suddenly blurted out, *"Ako muna. Ako muna ang aasikasuhin ni Mama bago kayo!"* **(I'm the first. Mama will attend to my needs first before she attends to your needs).** The children were so scared of him, so they just kept quiet.

I needed somebody to talk to and I thought my family could help me. So, I called up my sister, Weng, and told her everything that had happened. My sister was surprised with my revelation. She asked, *"Ading paano mo naitago ang lahat ng ito sa amin? Akala ko ba okay na kayo?"* **(Sister, how did you manage to hide everything from us? I thought you were all right?)**

Bearing the physical battering, emotional violence, and psychological torture was immensely challenging. If it were only me getting hurt, perhaps I would have endured every single thing, but my children in all their innocence were now traumatized. It was the lowest point in my life. That was my weakest and I had no recourse but to bend my knees in prayer and just allow the mighty power of God to work. He could have killed me that night but God sent his angels to protect me and my children. That was the time when God was strongest in my life.

LET US PRAY...

You made me strong to face all the physical, verbal, emotional, and psychological torture, and you have protected my children from harm. Thank you that instead of losing hope, you made me rise above my incapacity and discover my real strength that is in you, my Lord. Continue protecting us and may we be living witnesses of your salvific love to others. AMEN.

POINTS TO PONDER...

1. Have you ever been hurt verbally or physically by someone close to you? How did you feel?
2. How do you feel when someone accuses you of something you are innocent about?

3. If you encounter any form of violence, will you be violent in return? How do you think can this be avoided?

TALK TO GOD...

---

12 THE LIBERATING KISS OF JESUS

Pain and suffering have come to your life,
but remember pain, sorrow, suffering
are but the kiss of Jesus –
a sign that you have come so close to Him
that He can kiss you.
Mother Theresa

APRIL 6, 2003 WAS supposed to be our 12th year wedding anniversary. We used to celebrate our anniversary, but this time I purposely did not prepare. He was at the height of his depression. I informed my sister Weng, so that they will not expect anything a gathering.

On that day he did not want to go to Mass, so I and the kids left him at home. While we were in Church, my sister texted me saying they will be coming home for dinner. So, after the Mass, I dropped by the restaurant and bought some food. When we arrived home, Rod was not there. He was drinking alcohol with our neighbor. My sister and her family came, but he was not home yet.

After dinner, my brother-in-law, Dexter, invited him for a drink. He told Rod that depression caused by frustrations is normal. What matters is how we face these issues confronting us. My brother-in-law also encouraged him to join them in their Palawan trip during the Holy Week but he refused.

Every day of that Holy Week was really a week of passion for me. I had to watch my language and my actions so as not to trigger his anger. Any word I say, or any wrong move I do can elicit a negative response from him. I had to remind the kids every now and then to be quiet, not to play outside, and not to make any commotion.

Without his knowledge, I secretly packed a few clothes in the children's school bags. I was ready for anything to happen in case the situation worsened. Most of the time, I was quiet. I was praying and begging God for more courage, direction and guidance.

On Black Saturday, I went to Manila with the kids to pick up my sister and her family from Palawan. Our enjoyment was cut short by a text message from him saying MERALCO was there to cut our electric service. I told him to pay and instructed him to get the money from my blue bag. As expected he started to get angry and cursed at me, *"sana madisgrasya na kayo, sana mamatay na kayo, wag na kayong umuwi. Pag umuwi kayo, pagbababatuhin ko kayo.*" **(I wish you had an accident, I wish you'll all die, don't go home anymore. If you go home I will throw stones on you).** He even cursed my father, *"Mamatay na sana ang tatay mo.!* **(I wish your father dead).**

On our way home, he called and he talked to each of the children. The children would return the phone to me crying. When I asked them what he said, *"sabi po sana mamatay na daw tayo, sana madisgrasya na daw tayo.*" **(He said, he wished us dead, and he wished that we meet an accident).**

We went home to my sister's house. He started calling when we arrived. He continued to curse us, and every time I attempted to hang the phone he would bang his head and threatened that he would kill himself. He wanted us to go home that night.

Early the following day, Easter Sunday, I went to Mass early and asked for enlightenment. I talked to my sister after the Mass and decided to go back hoping that he is true to his promise that when we go home everything will be all right. We went home before lunch.

He opened the gate, he just looked at me angrily. He did not even bother to talk to the children. Out of fear that the kids might trigger his bad mood, I instructed the kids to stay in the room. I prepared lunch but he refused to eat.

At about 2:00 in the afternoon, he took a shower and left. He came back after an hour and asked what was there for lunch. I answered, *"Squid from Palawan."* He yelled, *"Tignan mo alam mo namang paborito ko yan ni hindi mo man lang ako niyaya?"* **(You see, you know that's my favorite but you did not even bother to invite me to eat?)** I just kept quiet and served him lunch.

After that, the whole house was quiet. Hay…. Thank God!

It was dinner time. As usual I prepared dinner for him. He got his food and ate in front of the TV. I served him coffee. He asked *"Para kanino yan?"* **(For whom is that?)** I said *"Papa sayo yan."* **(That's for you, Papa).** *"Bakit di mo sinasabi?"* **(Why did you not tell me?)** was his answer. I said softly *"Papa, tayo lang namang dalawa ang andito, kanino pa ba yan kundi sayo? Kaya nga nilagay ko sa harap mo."* **(Papa, we are only two here, so definitely that's yours. That's why I placed it in front of you).** Suspiciously he said *"Sigurado kang walang vetsin yan ha?"* **(Are you sure you it has no msg –monosodium glutamate?)**

He stood up, took the sugar canister and put four tablespoons of sugar into the cup while saying, *"Ito naman ang gusto mo di ba? Mamatay na ako?"* **(This is what you want, right? For me to die?)** Then he threw the spoon on the table in front of me. Not a single word came from my mouth.

He sat on the sofa and shouted at the top of his voice *"Putangina moooooo,"* **(Fuck you)** while throwing the mug of coffee at my direction. Good enough, it did not hit me. Trembling but quietly, I left my food, took the broom and the rag, and picked up the broken glasses. There was fear all over me, I was really shaking, I was so nervous. The kids and my nieces were in the room that time. They had no idea what was going on.

I went up to our room and instructed my nieces, CJ and Nina, to prepare their clothes--only the important ones. They were surprised, but without much explanation, I told them we will leave once there is an opportunity.

Early morning of April 21, 2003, I left the house with my four children. Rod was asleep. I woke the kids up and hurriedly but quietly, we prepared to leave. Without any fuss, I told them we will go to school for their enrolment.

The "great escape" happened that early morning. We passed through the back door for fear that he might be awakened by the sound of the metal gate. One of my friends, Rica, who also is our neighbor, helped us "escape." She hired a transportation for us. Ahhhh… that was an exodus.

He woke up when we were already at the SLEX, on our way to Manila. He was calling but I turned off my phone and changed my sim card. One of my friends, Carmen, offered her condominium unit in Makati. I and the kids, with Cathy, my niece who was taking care of Rocev, lived there for about a week.

My world was in a havoc. I reported everything that happened to the Police for documentation purposes. I visited the DVMI sisters at Mater Ecclesiae School where I found temporary solace and courage. They referred to me their psychistrist friend who lived in Alabang whom I could talk to.

Her advice was the same with the first doctor I consulted at CMC. Rod needed professional help the soonest time possible. And since she was a practicing psychiatrist in the US, she recommended that I go back to the one I talked to at CMC for advice on what to do.

Rod was diagnosed for bipolar disorder or manic depression at the UST Hospital and was treated for about ten days. While he was in the hospital, I also brought the children to another doctor for therapy because of the trauma they had with their father.

While Rod was still in the hospital, I happened to talk to one of my friends, Rita, who went through a similar experience with mine and he convinced me that it was time to break the cycle of violence in the family. She said the best time to do this was while he was in the hospital. *"If you don't want your children to grow up thinking that it is normal to hurt their partners in the future, you must separate now. If you really love yourself, decide now!"* This advice convinced me and gave me the boldness to finally flee away from all the pain.

I packed his things. I went to the hospital to pay his bills. On my way, Rica advised me, *"Emely kilala kita. Baka pag nakausap ka na naman ng biyenan mo ay wala ka na namang magawa sa plano mo. Dapat kang makaalis ng ospital bago pa sila dumating."* **(Emely, I know you. When you talk to your mother-in-law, you might not be able to execute your plans anymore. You must leave the hospital before they come).** She was right.

So, I placed all his clothes in a bag and entrusted it to the security guard. I wrote a short note to my mother-in-law. I told her I was so weary and exhausted that I needed much rest myself. I further said that I cannot take care of Rod yet, and that the children also need my attention and care. I gave his valuables to his doctor. I explained that my mother-in-law will bring him home and all bills were settled. While I was in the taxi going to the bus station, I sent my mother-in-law a message and informed her I entrusted Rod's stuff to the doctor and the security guard.

While I was in the bus to Calamba, my sister and some friends were busy packing our things because that very same night we were moving to my sister's house in Los Banos.

"Lord, why do I have to suffer this way? Have I done something wrong to deserve these?" My tears were just falling while I was in the bus. I was questioning the Lord. But I was reminded of Mother Theresa. Jesus must be kissing me. He must be embracing me. But it hurts because whenever he embraces me, the thorns on

His head also pierce me until it bleeds. The tighter He hugged and kissed me, the painful it became. But that was the most liberating kiss and embrace ever because it meant salvation for me.

Suffering is inevitable. If you look at the cross, you see His head bending down—He wants to kiss you, and He has both hands open wide because He wants to embrace you. He has his heart opened wide to receive you.

When you feel miserable inside, look at the cross and you will know what is happening. Suffering, pain, sorrow, humiliation, feelings of loneliness, are nothing but the kiss of Jesus, a sign that you have come so close that He can kiss you.

LET US PRAY...

Dear Jesus, it was so sweet of you to have kissed and embraced me, to have wrapped me in your arms and hugged me. But thank you that you were patient enough to understand me whenever I complained and almost quit during those times when you were kissing me. Thank you that you did not give up on me. Continue embracing me Lord, and as you hug me, may I learn to feel the pain and understand that with the pain comes glory and everlasting happiness. AMEN.

POINTS TO PONDER...

1. Have you ever complained to God for the seemingly unending trials in your life? Have you ever thought of just quitting?
2. But have ever experienced the deliverance of God after these sufferings? How did you feel?
3. Have you ever shared to others how God saved you from these trials?

TALK TO GOD…

---

13 GOD'S MY ROCK AND SALVATION

"My God, my rock, in whom I take refuge, my shield, and
the horn of my salvation,
my stronghold and my refuge, my savior;
you save me from violence.
I call upon the LORD,
who is worthy to be praised,
and I am saved from my enemies."
2 Samuel 22:3-4

HE CAN VISIT EVERY NOW AND THEN, he can
sleep over the weekend, but not live with us until such
time that he will be mentally and emotionally stable. That
was our arrangement because he did not want separation.
He always said, *"I want our family to be different from
my own family. All of my relatives are separated I don't
want this to happen to us."* I totally agreed.

On June 19, 2004, he came for a visit to Los Banos because
it was Racquel's birthday. He kept on saying that he wanted to

take the BAR examinations again and that this time he wanted to enroll in a review school. My ever understanding and considerate sister, Weng, convinced me, *"Sige na ading bigyan mo na baka yan ang makakapagbigay sa kanya ng fulfillment"* **(Go ahead, give him that might give him fulfillment).**

June 20, 2004, we agreed to meet at RCBC Calamba during lunch break to give him the money he needed for his BAR review. The whole morning while he was at home and I was in the office, he has been threatening me that he will make a scandal in Letran, and that he will look for the people who have been helping me, or if not he will kill me or my children. He was cursing everybody and even blaming God. Honestly, I got scared. So, I called my graduate student, Col. Chito for assistance. He said he will send some policemen to the campus during lunch in anticipation of what he might possibly do. That moment, I felt he was capable of inflicting harm on anyone.

While on my way to the bank, I got a call from Nina. She informed me that the security guards were in panic because some policemen were in school. I told her to please inform the security guards to stand by.

We met at RCBC. At the entrance, he already started making scenes by his loud voice and vulgar language. All the bank staff and clients inside were looking at us. I was so embarrassed that I just wanted to vanish that very moment. Good thing Engr. Bobadilla, the Engineering Department Dean was there. I whispered, *"Sir, please don't leave me." "Don't worry."* He assured me. *"Just follow me,"* he said.

As I was giving him the money he blurted out while looking at me fiercely, *"Gusto mo punutin ko yan?"* **(Do you want me to tear that apart?)** Upon hearing this, I hurriedly put the money in my pocket instead of giving it to him.

Dean Bobadilla and I hastily went out of the bank and boarded a jeepney. He also boarded the same. When we got off, he also got off. Then we took a tricycle to Letran. He took the same tricycle and sat at the back of the driver. While at the school gate, I could already see the policemen.

We got off at the main entrance. He immediately fled going to the second floor of the building. I and Dean Bobadilla were met by one of the policemen and we were escorted to the Rector's office. While the police officer was asking me questions, I received a call from Mylene informing me that Rod was in my office and he was looking for me.

I called Nina and Au and requested them to pick up my children from their classrooms. I was afraid that he might go to their classrooms and force the kids to go with him just like what he previously did. In a span of minutes, Nina and Au came with Renz, Racquel, and Reinier. We were all in the Rector's Boardroom trying to figure out what to do. We were supposed to have an Academic Board Meeting.

Fr. Stephen, our Secretary General, went to the Graduate School office and talked to him. Fr. Stephen later said that Rod's mood swing was very erratic. *"He was angry, shouting, cursing, and yelling at him for about 30 minutes, saying all kinds of bad words, then after that he was crying, a few minutes later, he was back to normal."* Fr. Stephen informed him that from that day on he was declared a *"persona non grata"* **(unwelcome person)** in Letran because of the trouble that he caused. Fr. Stephen also told me that had Rod hit him, he would not have second thoughts hitting him back. Good thing nothing physical happened between the two of them.

While Fr. Stephen and Rod were in my office, Fr. Audie, the former Treasurer of Letran, drove his car near the elevator. It was like a scene in an action movie. I, my kids, Au and Nina were escorted by one security guard and one police officer down to the ground floor. When the elevator opened, the security guard made sure that Rod was not there. He looked at his left and right, and said while gesturing his hand for us to go out, *"Ma'am, ok po. Pwede po."* **(Okay Ma'am. You may go.)** And we all ran and hopped quickly into Fr. Audie's car.

We managed to leave the school premises. We were brought to Nina's house, a private resort in Pansol. My children did not have the whole idea of what was going on. I pitied them and I was crying inside. I was so confused. I didn't know what to do. Thank God my friends were there to cheer me up and take care of the children while I was so disoriented. I couldn't believe all these things were happening to us.

I called up my sister immediately and told her to go home and bring Rocev and Cathy to her office. I was afraid that Rod will go home and hurt them. My sister did. Good enough that before he got home, Rocev and Cathy were already in Ate Weng's office.

Rod called up my sister and asked permission if he can go inside the house. My sister allowed him to enter for fear that he might get angry. That same night, I asked Col. Chito to send some policemen to secure my sister's house because my sister was afraid to go home with him in the house.

My sister went home and begged him to leave. It took time before he was convinced. He was escorted by the police to the hospital because suddenly he complained about his kidney. My sister thought that he was just acting out. He came back the following day and told my sister that he will just sleep for a while then he will go home to Tarlac.

We spent the night at Nina's house. The following day was the Graduate School's graduation. I felt like floating in the air. I asked my niece, CJ, to bring me some clothes and a pair of shoes, including my toga/academic gown for the graduation. Every now and then, my sister would send me messages to update me on what was going on at home.

We were all ready for the graduation but the tension was there. The funny thing was that some parents were wondering whether any VIP was coming because there was tight security in the campus. Fr. Stephen explained that since it was the first exclusive Graduate School graduation, they wanted it safe and special for everyone.

When the graduation song started to play, I heard my phone alert. A text message from my sister said, *"Ading, salamat sa Diyos. Umalis na siya. Inihatid siya ni Nina sa sakayan ng bus."* **(Sister, thank God. He left. Nina brought her to the bus stop).** I took a deep breath and said a short prayer, *"Salamat sa Diyos!"* **(Thank God!)** We started marching.

During the graduation rites, my happiness was overflowing. My mind continued to marvel at the miracles that have happened in my life in a matter of two days. But at that point, I can't help but think about what's going to happen next. The sufferings and struggles seemed endless.

But once again, God has made His presence so alive. He has again proven that in Him, nothing is impossible. He is my rock and my salvation, therefore whom shall I fear? He has saved me and my family from violence! He is indeed worthy to be praised and glorified.

LET US PRAY...

Ever living God, you have once again proven that you are indeed alive and in control of everything that is happening in our lives. Time and again, you have reminded me that you are indeed alive and in control of everything that is happening in our lives. Time and again, you have reminded me that you are my rock and in you I have nothing to fear because you are my salvation. Continue protecting me and my family from any harm, deliver us from every evil, and bring us to everlasting life. AMEN. you are my rock and in you I have nothing to fear because you are my salvation. Continue protecting me and my family from any harm, deliver us from every evil, and bring us to everlasting life. AMEN.

POINTS TO PONDER...

1. Have you ever experienced escaping from danger, or evade a risk to your life or someone else's life?
2. Have you ever been humiliated or embarrassed in public?
3. What did you do during those times? To whom did you turn to?

TALK TO GOD...

____

____

____

14 CHILDREN ARE GOD'S PRECIOUS GIFTS

Behold, children are a gift of the LORD,
The fruit of the womb is a reward.
Psalm 127:3

"MAMA, PAKISUNDAN PO *yang kotse na iyan.* *Yung nasa harapan mo,"* (Mr. Driver, please follow that car. That car in front of you). **"Ay bakit po? Kilala niyo po ba siya?"** (Why? Do you know him?) **he asked. "Opo. Mga anak ko po ang nasa loob ng kotse."** (Yes. My children are inside the car). **The three teenagers in the jeepney looked at me and got some pipes under the chair. "Sige po tutulungan namin kayo,"** (Ok. We will help you) **they offered. "Ay naku huwag. Ako na ang bahala. Salamat!"** (No. I can manage. Thank you!) **I was trembling with fear all over.**

When we reached Pansol, a resort area where traffic is really out of control, all cars were in full stop. I got all the coins in my bag, without even counting how much it was, handed it

119

to the driver, *"Mama ito po ang bayad. Bababa na po ako."* **(Mr. Driver, here's my payment. I will get off here)** and without waiting for his answer, I jumped off the jeepney.

I hurriedly ran and stood in front of the car, raised my arms, and stopped them. I did not care at all if they will run over me, or people who know me will see me. All the vehicles were blowing their horns because we were causing more traffic. All bystanders were looking at us. We became the center of attention. I did not mind or care for anything at all, except for my children's safety. So, they had no choice but to let me hop inside the car.

Have you seen this Robin Padilla or Sharon Cuneta movie before? No! It was not a movie, not a telenovela, not a drama series, not even a shooting. It was not for *"reel"* but it was for *"real."*

When this happened, I just assumed my new office as Dean of the Arts and Sciences Department, aside from being the Dean of the Graduate School.

June 4, 2003 at about 12 noon while I was busy for the enrolment in my office, my phone rang. *"Mama,"* it was Renz on the phone. *"Tumawag po si Papa tinanong niya kung pwede daw ba kaming kumain sa Jollibee. Noong sinabi kong opo ibinaba niya agad yung phone. Mama feeling ko andito lang siya sa malapit,"* **(Papa called and asked if we can eat at Jollibee. When I said yes, he hanged the phone immediately. Mama, I feel he is just around** *nearby.)* I could feel fear from her voice. I was beginning to break down. *"Anak, please huwag kayong lalabas ng bahay, huwag kayong sasama kahit na anong mangyari. Antayin niyo ako."* **(Child, please don't go out of the house, don't go with him whatever happens. Wait for me).** I took my bag and left my office. I rushed home.

True enough, he, together with his brother and uncle, went to my sister's house and took my three children, Renz, Racquel, and Reinier without my permission. He left Rocev who was only two years old then. While I was on my way home, I received a call from my niece, Lei-anne, *"Tita kinuha po ni Tito Rod ang mga bata. Naka kotse sila. Ang bilis nilang umalis pero nakuha namin ang plate number ng kotse."* **(Tita, Tito Rod took the children. They were in a car. They quickly left but we got the plate number of the car.)**

When I heard this, I immediately got off the jeepney and while I was crossing the street, a speedy car passed right in front of me. I looked at the plate number, it was exactly the plate number given to me by my niece. My heart began beating fast as my fear and ancxiety was starting to build.

Thanks to the traffic in Pansol, Calamba, Laguna, I was able to catch them.

The one driving the car was his brother, and the one seated in front was his uncle. The three kids were at the back seat with Rod. I sat beside him. They were not crying but I could see the panic in their eyes. I felt they wanted to cry, but they were afraid that their Papa will scold them. They were in their play clothes, slippers, and haven't taken a bath. Then Rod started shouting at the top of his voice. That was the time when they began to cry.

They wanted to drop me off at Crossing, Calamba but I refused. Then we stopped at Star Gasoline Station at SLEX to buy some food. We had a chance to talk, though he was making some scenes because of his booming voice and crass language. He wanted me to go to Tarlac with him, he wanted me to resign from Letran, he wanted me to give up my position in the school. Just to pacify him and to avoid any further scandal in public, I agreed to what he wanted to happen.

When we were back in the car, Rod informed his brother that we will get off at Alabang because he was going back to Los Banos with us. His brother got furious and shouted at him, *"hihingi hingi ka ng tulong tapos magbabago ang isip mo? Bahala ka sa buhay mo. Hindi ka na namin tutulungan."* **(You asked for help and now you changed your mind? It's up to you. We will not help you anymore).**

That very instant, Rod changed his mind. We were like two crazy people texting each other inside the car. In his message he said, *"nagbago na ang isip ko, dadalhin ko ang mga bata, bumaba ka na. Hihintayin kita sa Sunday."* **(I changed my mind, I will bring the kids, get off here. I will wait for you on Sunday).** He instructed his brother to stop the car. I was so helpless, I could not do anything. They forcibly dropped me off at the intersection of Santolan and EDSA. While getting off, I saw my children crying, reaching out their arms, showing that they wanted to go with me. It was heart-wrenching!

I sat along the road and cried my heart out. That moment, I felt that I was about to lose my consciousness. People were looking at me but what they thought of didn't bother. I was only thinking of my children.

When I regained my senses, I took a jeepney and went to my cousin's house in 4th West Crame. There, I cried again and told her the whole story. I called my sister and she encouraged me to go home.

I went to Los Baños Police to report what happened on June 5, 2003. They advised me to file a case of kidnapping against his brother and uncle but I decided otherwise because it will only complicate matters. I was listless for a few days. Good thing my sister was there to encourage me. She convinced me not to worry because Rod will not hurt the kids. They are his children, too.

I decided not to go to Tarlac for fear that he might hurt me again. My sister talked to him over the phone and convinced him to bring the children back because June 7 was the opening of classes. Indeed, he brought the kids back that Sunday afternoon. They traveled all the way from Tarlac to Los Banos in slippers and it was a good thing that he bought some clothes for them, bringing with them their soiled clothes in plastic bags.

When I saw them, I cried and thanked God for they all came back safe and unhurt.

At that point, I was ready to sacrifice anything and everything for my children even it would mean my own death. When I stood in front of the car, I was ready to die for them. Had his brother put on the accelerator, I could have died. I was all ready for it. But then again, it was God Himself who saved me and His precious gifts, His very own children, the fruits of my womb.

LET US PRAY...

Dear Lord, thank you for taking care of my children, for keeping them away from any injury, and most of all thank you for protecting them especially their emotions which are very fragile and sensitive. Thank you for giving them to me as your most precious gifts. Continue blessing them in their careers and in their future professions. Give them the best persons who will love them, who will accept them, and form a family that they will live with for the rest of their lives. AMEN.

POINTS TO PONDER...

1. How far have you shown your love to your children/family members?
2. Up to what extent have you fought for your children's/family members' well-being?

3. How do you plan to continue strengthening your relationship with your children/relatives/family members?

TALK TO GOD…

____

____

____

____

15 GOD FIGHTS THE BATTLE FOR YOU

"You will not need to fight in this battle.
Stand firm, hold your position, and see the
salvation of the LORD on your behalf,
O Judah and Jerusalem.'
Do not be afraid and do not be dismayed.
Tomorrow, go out against them,
and the LORD will be with you."
2 Chronicles 20:17

**ONE OF THE READERS of "And God Smiled
Back," who happens to be one of Rod's aunts and
confidant, sent me these questions: "Got some questions
Ems…What year did you separate? What year did you
take the kids to Ilocos? How old are they? What grade are**

they? When did you bring them back to Laguna? When did you become the Dean? What happened in the Holy Week of 2004, before you got the email?"

I answered all the questions except the last one – *"What happened in the Holy Week of 2004, before you got your email?"* She was referring to the 11th chapter entitled *"My Resurrection Experience."* At the end of our chat, I said, *"Auntie, by the way, may isang tanong ka na di ko pa nasagot. I prefer to answer it in person. Yung what happened before the Holy Week of 2004."* **(Auntie, by the way, you have one question which I have not answered yet. I prefer to answer it in person. That on what happened before the Holy Week of 2004).** Unfortunately, we had no chance to meet anymore.

So, this is what happened in the Holy Week of 2004. These are excerpts from the testimony I submitted in court when I filed my annulment.

April 4, 2004, Rod arrived to attend CJ's (my niece) graduation. We had a very simple celebration in a resort. My family treated him well, as if nothing has happened and everything was usual. In fact my father even called him to join us prepare our food. He was part of the family. He was happy. In fact, he jammed with us in the videoke. I thought everything will be perfectly all right.

We arrived home at about 10 o'clock in the evening, still in a very festive atmosphere, until he shouted at the top of his voice, *"Ma!!!"* I always felt frantic whenever I hear this loud voice. I hurriedly approached him. I didn't know that my father was behind me and witnessed Rod hitting me on my knee. For the very first time my father got furious. Rod immediately knelt before my father and asked for forgiveness. *"Tata, sorry patawarin niyo po ako. Hindi ko sinasadya."* **(Father, I'm sorry. I didn't mean to do it.)** My father, with a firm voice said, *"Rod tumayo ka. Hindi ako Diyos para luhuran mo. Nirerespeto kita dahil matalino kang tao. Madami ng problemang dumaan sa inyong mag-asawa pero wala kang narinig sa akin. Ngayon lang. Sino ang nagbigay sayo ng karapatan na saktan ang anak ko? Ako mismo ni hindi ko siya napagbuhatan ng kamay"* **(Rod, stand up. I am not God for you to kneel before me. I respect you because you are an intelligent person. There have been a lot of problems that you and your wife went through but you did not hear anything from me. It's only now that I am saying this, but who gave you the right to hurt my daughter? I, myself, have never hit her.)**

That night I observed many unusual things about Rod's behavior. He was persistently looking for his belt which he said was just in the room. I just let him.

Then, he took his shirt and told me that he was leaving. I immediately said yes. Then he said *"Hindi kaya sila magagalit?"* **(Will they not get angry?)**

After a few seconds, he was looking intently at the shirt and asked *"kanino yan?"* **(Whose is that?).** I told him that the shirt was his and he answered *"hindi ah, hindi sa akin yan."* **(No, that's not mine)**.

He stood at the door of our room and measured it through the use of his arms saying *"Ma, bakit parang ang laki ng pintuan natin?"* **(Ma, why does the door look big?)**.

While seated he was looking intently at the door where there was a crucifix and began to smile. When I asked him why he was smiling, he answered *"Inaalala ko lang kung sinong madre ang nagbigay niyan."* **(I am just recalling who was the nun who gave that)**.

Then he began to take hold of a pair of scissors, but he started to look for a sharper one. Then, he got a pointed nail cutter and put it in his pocket. Later, he returned it back.

So unexpectedly that he joined together two electrical cords/extension cords and placed it beside him.

Rod's actions made me so agitated and suspicious so I asked my sister, Weng, not to leave us. Besides, he did not want to sleep. And when we told him to sleep, he said he wanted to take a shower at 4 o'clock in the morning. Finally, he fell asleep at 6 o'clock.

That morning I informed my father about my final decision to separate from him temporarily otherwise I will go crazy or put myself and the children in danger. I would like to talk to him in the presence of the whole family. My father agreed. So, when he woke up, we had a family meeting. My father said, *"Rod, ayusin mo na ang mga gamit mo. Isasabay ka na namin pauwing Ilocos. Ihahatid ka namin sa Mommy mo para magusap kami."* **(Rod, fix your things. You will ride with us to Ilocos. We will drop you at your Mom's place so that we can talk."**

He looked at me. With a low but firm voice I said, *"Pa, ayusin mo na muna ang sarili mo. Dito muna kami ng mga bata, huwag mo kaming alalahanin. Pag maayos ka na, magusap uli tayo. Hindi natin paguusapan ang hiwalayan."* **(Pa, settle yourself first. I and the kids will stay here. Don't worry about us. When you are okay, let us talk again. We will not talk about separation.)**

Rod begged, *"Ma, paano ako? Hindi ko kaya na mawala kayo."* **(Ma, what about me? I cannot live without you.)** I answered, *"Hindi kami mawawala sa iyo. Gusto ko lang munang magpahinga. Pagod na pagod na ako."* **(We will not leave you. I just want to rest. I'm very tired).**

Then I stood, turned my back and went inside my sister's house without looking back at him.

After that talk, Rod went back to our room. We thought he was already packing his things. When I peeped into our room, I saw him hanging his belt at the door. Then, my brother-in-law saw him lying in bed with the belt beside him. He was alone in the room. I started praying that nothing wrong will happen. I texted my friends and requested for prayers.

At about 2 o'clock in the afternoon, while everybody was busy preparing to leave for Ilocos, we heard a loud scream. My brother and brother-in-law rushed to our room. Rod has locked the door. My brother had to break and pass over the wall to be able to get inside. Rod was seen with his head between the bed railings, with two belts around his neck (the other belt belonged to my son) banging his head on the wall. A note was also seen in the room with the following message written:

Mahal na mahal ko kayong lahat. Sana patawarin mo ako sa lahat ng nagawa ko. Wag mo pababayaan ang mga bata. Wala talaga ako mapuntahan kundi sa pamilya ko. **(I love you all. I hope that you can forgive me with what I did. Don't neglect the children. I have nothing to turn to except my family).**

My brother and brothers-in-law rushed him to Los Banos Doctor's Hospital (LBDH). Right after the incident, my sister called up his mother and brother. They promised to come the following day.

Despite what happened, my father, with all patience and understanding, encouraged us to visit him in the hospital. *"Tatay pa rin siya ng mga anak mo. Dapat niyang makita ang mga anak niya"* **(He is still your children's father. He has to see them),** he advised. Inspite of our hesitation to go because the children, especially Renz who was so frightened, we obeyed. Renz was trembling in fear because she saw her father being rushed to the hospital, but with my assurance that nothing will happen to her, I brought her close to Rod and he embraced her, saying he was sorry.

The doctors made him sleep so that he can rest. Rod has not been sleeping for several days now. We were informed by the doctors that he might be very strong physically when he wakes up and recovers. So we requested the hospital attendants to take care of him.

The following day, April 5, 2004, it was Holy Monday, my sister received a text message from my mother-in-law telling her she is not going to visit him. My sister called her up and begged that Rod be taken to Tarlac. We knew that he was asleep so we felt relieved and relaxed. The tension in the house subsided.

April 6, 2004, Holy Tuesday, was our 13th wedding anniversary, but we did not celebrate. There was nothing to celebrate. Rod was still asleep in the hospital as the doctors and the nurses kept us informed of his condition.

On April 7, 2004, Holy Wednesday, I got a call from the hospital to tell us that my mother-in-law visited Rod at around

3 o'clock in the afternoon. She left that same afternoon without calling to even say "hello" to me, the children or to my family.

April 8, 2004, Holy Thursday, we expected that my mother-in-law would return to settle the hospital bills, because that was what she promised Rod's doctor, and that she was to make an arrangement for an ambulance to bring Rod back to Tarlac. She never came back.

I and my sister had no choice but to settle the hospital bills. We also hired a van to bring him home to Tarlac and I requested for two military escorts from Col. Chito. He left LBDH at around 1:30 in the afternoon. I chose not see him anymore. When they left, I and my sister felt solace. Finally, we were liberated from all the worry, stress, and tension.

When they were in Manila, one of the police escorts sent me a message informing me that they had to drop by the Victory Liner bus terminal to pick up my mother-in-law. She went back with them to Tarlac.

On their way home to Tarlac, Rod sent me a text message to thank me and he promised to return the money I spent for his hospitalization. He also sent a text message to my sister saying *"pagbalik ko, maipagmamalaki na ninyo ako"* **(When I return, you'll be proud of me.)**

April 9, 2004, Good Friday, I spent my day at home with my children. I felt like I was joining Christ in His passion and in

His sufferings leading to His crucifixion in Mount Calvary. I spent my day in prayer, *"Lord, my suffering is nothing compared to your sufferings. Your sacrifices are greater than mine. But, Lord, human as I am, I cannot bear any more. Please, take this cup away from me. Spare me from more pains. But your will be done."*

The Lord reminded me, *"You will not need to fight in this battle. Stand firm, hold your position, and see the salvation of the Lord on your behalf. Do not be afraid and do not be dismayed. Tomorrow, go out against them, and the LORD will be with you."*

And the Lord, indeed, is faithful. He keeps His promises. He won the battle for me.

It was on Easter Monday, April 11, 2004, that I received my acceptance email as one of the Research Fellows of the Korea Foundation for Advanced Studies (KFAS). After the suffering, passion, death and resurrection, came the best Easter experience of my life--a new life has come!

God has won the battle for me. All I had to do was trust that His salvation will come. The fear in me was fought with faith in my heart. He never left me. I died with him but I also resurrected with Him.

LET US PRAY...

Thank you, Lord for sustaining me with your power when I was going through this passion in my life. Thank you for sending me my family and friends who have become the source of my courage to fight and to have faith in you. Thank you, God for winning this battle for me. May you always remind me that there is no mountain too tall that you cannot move, and that there is no storm too strong that you cannot calm. AMEN.

POINTS TO PONDER...

1. When was the time you were most helpless and just surrendered everything to God?
2. Where do you normally draw your strength in times of sufferings in your life?
3. Were you ever hopeless and felt like giving up? What did you do?

TALK TO GOD...

____

____

____

16 GOD'S PERFECT PLAN

"I know the plans I have in mind for you,
declares the LORD;
they are plans for peace, not disaster,
to give you a future filled with hope.
Jeremiah 29:11

AFTER FOUR YEARS of being a missionary at the
Filipino Community in Seoul, I was contemplating on
finally going home to the Philippines and be with my
children. I was also thinking that while I still have
a *"market value,"* I'd better go back and begin to look for
work in the academe where my passion really was.

I was all set into this decision when, in one basketball event
of the community, I met the former Ambassador to South
Korea, Amb. Luis Cruz, and he mentioned, *"Doc Emely, there is
one university that is recruiting Filipino students. I will send you the contact*

information." The next day, I got the contact information and without any second thoughts, I called up.

But nobody answered my call. *"I will call again later,"* I resolved. After a few minutes, my phone rang. What appeared in the screen was the number I just called a few minutes ago. *"Hello!"* I excitedly greeted. *"Hello, did you phone me,"* the person at the other line asked. *"Ah yes. I am Prof. Emely Abagat. I called because our Philippine Ambassador mentioned that you are recruiting Filipino students,"* I slowly explained. *"Oh yes! We do. And may I know who is applying?"* he inquired. *"I am thinking if my daughter who is in the university could apply,"* I said. He immediately answered, *"I'm sorry our programs are not for undergraduate students. They are for graduate students."*

When I heard the words *"graduate students,"* my excitement mounted up. *"Really? How about post-doctoral students? Are they eligible to apply?"* I inquired. *"Why? Who wants to take a post-doctoral course?"* he asked. *"I am interested!"* I said. *"Why don't you apply as a professor? We are also recruiting foreign professors."* When I heard this, I felt the whole world brighten. *"Really? I can apply as a professor!"* I enthusiastically remarked.

Then I realized I was talking to the Dean of International Affairs. He instructed me to send my Curriculum Vitae immediately and invited me to visit his office for an interview the following Monday. At that time I could not contain my happiness. *"Lord, what is this again? Don't you want me to leave Korea?"* After agreeing on the interview date and time, and after thanking him for the opportunity that rarely comes in a lifetime, I decided to end our conversation.

But before I can say goodbye he asked me, *"Excuse me. What's your full name again?"* he curiously queried. *"Professor, I am Emely Dicolen-Abagat,"* I answered. *"Wait a moment,"* he continued. *"Your name sounds familiar. Were you on radio a few days ago? I think I heard you talking about the issue of migration in Korea,"* he said. I felt like I was in heaven. *"Yes, Professor! I was on TBS-EFM radio last week. And yes! I was interviewed,"* I excitedly affirmed him. *"Yes, I'm right! You are the same person I was* 

A radio interview at TBS-EFM Radio on the topic "Filipino Migration in Korea."

listening to while I was driving my car. I turned on my car stereo and it was you on the radio. Oh, what a coincidence!" he said. *"See you then on Monday!"* he hanged the phone.

This phone conversation gave me a feeling of ecstasy, and since I was alone in my room at the seminary of the Korean Missionary Society (KMS) where I was teaching that time, I shouted and jumped for your joy. This is another unexpected blessing from God.

Monday afternoon came. I was already at the office of the Dean of International Affairs. I brought with me my CV and other documents. I prepared two copies and I was ready for anything that could happen. After introducing ourselves personally to each other, he offered me a seat and he called someone over the phone. A few minutes later, another guy came in the room and he was introduced as the Dean of Academic Affairs.

The Dean of International Affairs explained about their program for the recruitment of Filipino graduate students. He asked me about the possible strategies to be able to get the best students to help in the "internationalization" program of the university. I honestly shared my opinion. After that, the Dean of Academic Affairs said in Korean (which I understood a bit), *"I like her pronunciation. She can apply as a professor."* The Dean of International Affairs said, *"That's why she is here. I invited her to apply and I think she is ready with her documents."* I handed them a folder of my CV. They browsed through it. They invited me for the final interview. The Academic Dean said they will send an email for the schedule of the interview. I could not believe myself that these were happening to me. I knew God was at work.

True enough! The next day I received an email telling me about the schedule of the interview. I was also informed that all the Deans will be in the panel including the University President. When I read this, I wanted to back out. Never, in my entire career, have I experienced being interviewed for a job with this kind of panel. I was so nervous. What was surprising though was that they gave me a set of questions to prepare for the interview: *How can we invite Filipino graduate students to our university? What possible approaches can we use to recruit? Which possible universities can we visit?* These were the questions I remember. I was expected to answer all these questions in 20 minutes. After 20 minutes, the panel members will ask different questions for another 20 minutes.

It was my first time to be interviewed by a Korean university so I had no idea how things would go. What I had in mind was how I interviewed my faculty applicants when I was a Dean at Letran Calamba. But over the weekend, I thought of a better way of presenting my ideas. I prepared a powerpoint presentation answering all the questions as clearly as possible. At least, if I have visuals, my answers will be more organized. A PPT will serve as my *"idiot board,"* I thought.

When I arrived at the interview venue, I peeped into the room and I saw one applicant doing a demonstration lesson using the powerpoint. *"Yes! I made the right decision to make a presentation for myself!"* I saw around 20 people in the room. I got scared. I was asked to wait for a few minutes outside the room. While waiting, I prayed for enlightenment, for courage to face the panel members, and the confidence to answer all their questions correctly.

With the empowerment of the Holy Spirit, my presentation went well. I was a bit anxious in the beginning, especially when

I saw the administrators waiting for what I had to say. But as I went on, I mustered the courage I needed and my powerpoint presentation served its purpose well. Twenty minutes passed minutes so quickly. I was confident I answered all their questions satisfactorilyout .

After twenty minutes of Q and A, I went down the platform and the Dean of Academic Affairs thanked me for an excellent presentation. He handed me a box of university business cards saying, *"Here's your business card. You can use this in promoting our university. Please wait for our phone call."* I said thank you and left the room.

When I was going out of the building, I curiously took the box of business cards out from my bag and read what was written down. What struck me was ***"Prof. Emely Dicolen-Abagat!"*** My name was written on it. How could this be? I just had my interview and how come I was given these business cards with my name on it? I was completely puzzled. A part of me was saying, *"Hey, congratulations!"* But another part of me was saying, *"Don't be too confident!"*

When I got off the shuttle bus, I went to the coffee shop and composed myself. The first person I called was my sister, Weng, and told her about the whole experience. She was as excited as I was but she said we'd better wait for the final result. Then I called my daughter, Renz. She assured me, *"Ma, I'm sure you are already accepted. Those business cards mean that the interview today was just a formality."* I still could not believe it. But perhaps she was right.

I continued my travel home still wondering about the final result. After about an hour, while I was in the subway, my phone rang, *"Hello!"* he said. I immediately recognized the voice at the other line. *"Congratulations! You did great during the interview. I know I am not in a position to reveal the final results, but… you are 99% accepted,"* he informed. I wanted to shout for joy but I was in a crowded subway. He continued, *"It's only 99% because as you mentioned you are scheduled to go home to the Philippines. So, you have a mission. Since you are going ahead of us, may we ask you to help us in our recruitment program for Filipino students? Please see us before you leave."*

My plan was to go back to the academe in the Philippines. I never imagined applying in a Korean university because I thought my credentials were not at par with other foreign and Korean professors. But God has His own plans for me. God has His own ways. One thing for sure, the radio interview that the International Affairs Dean heard was not at all accidental, it was providential.

Indeed, God has better plans for us and he surprises us with His plans. These are plans that will bring us peace and prosperity, plans that will not devastate us. He is in charge. We just have to allow him to be totally in control with our lives.

LET US PRAY...

Dear God, I feel so unworthy of all these surprises. I don't deserve them, Lord, but you keep on showering me with your love. Forgive me that many times I insist on my plans and rely on my own efforts, yet you patiently guide me and continue to unfold your ever greater plans for me. Grant me the grace to be always open to your promptings and allow you to move into my life. AMEN.

POINTS TO PONDER...

1. What future plans do you have in mind? Career? Family? Moving? Finances?
2. Do you consider God's will when making plans? How do you know it is God's will?
3. Has God ever surprised you with something you did not expect? How did you feel?

TALK TO GOD...

____

____

____

____

____

17 THE MAGIC WORD – "SORRY!"

"If your brother offends you,
take him to task about it,
and if he is sorry, forgive him.
Yes, if he wrongs you seven times in one day
and turns to you and says,
'I am sorry' seven times, you must forgive him."
Luke 17:3-4

IT WAS A SUNNY DAY on April 6, 1991 at the Santa Maria Goretti Parish Church also known as **Pope Pius XII Catholic Center in Manila. The banquet was held at the Casa Blanca of Casa Manila in Intramuros. All the guests wore smiles on their faces, praying and wishing only the best for two special people who will be joined in Matrimony.**

Wedding picture taken on April 6, 1991 at the Sta. Maria Goretti Parish Church, UN Avenue, Manila.

It was the most memorable day of my life because that was the day when my husband and I exchanged our *"I do's."* I vividly remember when he said sweetly during our exchange of vows, **"Emely, my sweetheart, take this ring as a sign of my love and my loyalty. In the name of the Father, and of the Son, and of the Holy Spirit."** After this, we heard the guests cheer, **"Wow! So sweet!"** To be wedded to the one you dearly love, witnessed by people close to your heart is the best thing that could ever happen to a woman whose dream is to have a united, happy family.

I was already teaching then and my husband was a full time senior student at a Law School in Manila. Though I was the only one working at that time, we were able to manage our finances as we lived a simple, quiet life. Our eldest child was born after a year of our marriage and we were able to move to our own small house before she turned one year old. At that time, I could not ask for anything more.

After he finished Law School, my husband was given the opportunity to teach in the same school where I was teaching. He was famous among the students because he was such a great, smart, and good-looking teacher. For me, that was a compliment and I was proud of him. Students in our campus looked up to us as a model couple. Though we had little arguments and small differences at times, we were able to patch it up immediately before the end of the day.

Then came our second child in 1995. We were both delighted for the added blessing to our family. I considered the first five years of my marriage *"heaven."* I thought our relationship was getting stronger and deeper. I never imagined that a 'storm' will come to rock the peaceful waters in our marriage.

One day in July of 1996, this peace and harmony was disrupted by a young lady who had an affair with my husband. She was both my Moral Theology student and my husband's Labor Relations student. It was a celebrated case in our college. Consequently, the student was kicked-out of school and my husband was asked to resign from work. I was totally devastated. The impact of his misbehavior to me and my family was unimaginable. This almost caused our marital breakdown.

The ordeal did not end there. I discovered that my husband brought the young lady home to my mother-in-law's house in Tarlac. She accepted both of them in her house, and kept it a secret from me. I made a surprise visit, together with Madeleine, one of our "Ates" who took care of my children, and true enough the young lady was there with my husband right inside my mother-in-law's bedroom.

The very sight of the young lady and my husband with my mother-in-law in her very room shattered me to pieces. *"How could these three people cheat and betray me?"* I felt the whole world crush on me. That time I was pregnant with Reinier, my third and eldest son. It was the first time in my life that I felt rage and hatred in my heart.

This resentment, I carried in my heart for seventeen years. Seventeen long years.

After some time, Madeleine came to visit. She recalled that incident when we went to my mother-in-law's place, traveling from Los Banos at midnight to arriving at Tarlac around 5 o'clock in the morning. There we took them by surprise--my husband, the young lady and my mother-in-law. We excitedly recalled how I collared and pushed the young lady on the floor because of my anger and disgust. While Madeleine and I were trying to recall what had happened then, I was trying to figure my feelings and sentiments of the moment. Surprisingly, the pain and the bitterness was gone. I used to cry or get furious when I remember this incident. But now, I can laugh at it and can't help but wonder how I was able to push her down on the floor despite my delicate condition.

After that visit, a thought came to me. I started to search for the young lady's Facebook account and became curious of what might have happened to her. I've seen her profile picture years back because we had a common friend, but there was still anger in my heart back then.

However, this time upon opening her Facebook page, I saw the photos of her cute children. Honestly, I only felt happiness for her, She now has a family of her own. I was pleased because regardless of what happened to her, somebody offered her true love and acceptance. Based on the photos I saw, it seems she is happily married, gifted with a very responsible and loving husband.

In my heart I said *"Thank God she was spared from a miserable life."* I thought of sending her a personal message. But before that, I prayed. *"Dear God, you know my intentions. If she answers, I will be glad. If she does not, then help me accept it."*

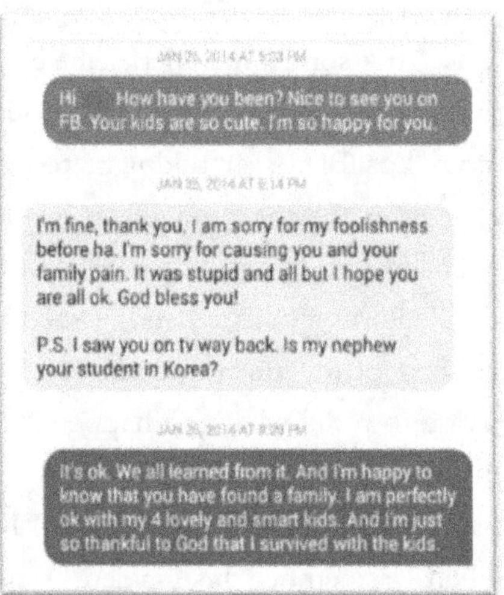

Sincerely I wrote *"Hi Gay! How have you been? Nice to see you on FB. Your kids are so cute. I'm so happy for you."*

To my surprise, after about an hour, I got a reply. It said, *"I'm fine, thank you. I am sorry for my foolishness before ha. I'm sorry for causing you and your family pain. It was stupid and all but I hope you are all ok. God bless you!"*

I smiled and my heart rejoiced. The magic word *"sorry"* liberated me from the slavery of pain.

Without hesitation I replied, *"It's ok. We all learned from it. And I'm happy to know that you have found a family. I am perfectly ok with my four lovely and smart kids. And I'm just so thankful to God that I survived with them."*

The hurt and bad memories buried in my heart for seventeen years disappeared instantaneously. Suddenly, I was free from the pain, anger, bitterness and un-forgiveness. I felt God's embrace and compassion have totally healed me from my brokeness.

Sigh…. Thank you God for the gift of humility and forgiveness.

Looking back, I realized that she must have also suffered from this experience. She must also have had pains in her relationship with my husband. Coming from a broken family herself, she witnessed her parent's separation. She grew up under the care of her grandmother who pampered her with money to compensate for the absence of her parent's love. She might have been looking for true love and acceptance at that young age of eighteen when her affair with my husband happened.

I remember that when her uncle and aunt met with me to apologize on behalf of their niece, they said, *"Don't worry she has no love to give your husband because she, herself, is in need of love. How can she love when she does not know how to love herself?"*

When I returned to Korea, I narrated this story to one of my friends. With her sweet smile and her compassionate embrace I felt it was Jesus embracing and whispering to me, *"Emely, you did a great job. That is exactly the meaning of love and forgiveness."* I have no more tears, I have no more pains because I have been liberated from the slavery of resentments. I have also realized two things: First, I must apologize to her and second, I have to thank her as well.

I must say sorry to her. Sorry for what? I must say sorry because in some ways I may have hurt her, not only physically, but emotionally too, because I failed to understand her.

I must thank her. Thank her for what? I must thank her because from this experience I learned to be closer to God, I became stronger, and I learned to forgive.

Yes, time heals all the wounds and erases the scars in our heart. But for healing to take place, we should have the humility to forgive ourselves and others. Forgiveness doesn't happen once, twice or thrice, but is a life-long challenge of letting go, of loving continuously, of accepting unconditionally because this is what God wants us to do.

LET US PRAY...

Oh most loving Jesus, you know how I felt. It was not at all easy to forgive someone who have hurt you and bruised you all over. But you made everything possible so that your name be glorified. Thank you for sparing this girl from misery and giving her someone who accepted her and gave her a better life. I know she was broken, too. Lord, I pray, that as we both move on with our lives, may this be a learning experience for us and be shared to others, not to put each other down, but to give you praise and glory. AMEN.

POINTS TO PONDER...

1. Has anyone cheated on you? How did you feel?
2. How did you manage to settle your differences with the other person involved?
3. What made it difficult for you to forgive?

TALK TO GOD...

____

____

____

18 WORRY NOT

"Therefore I tell you,
do not worry about your life,
what you will eat or drink; or about your body,
what you will wear. Is not life more than food,
and the body more than clothes?
Look at the birds of the air; they do not sow or reap or
store away in barns,
and yet your heavenly Father feeds them.
Are you not much more valuable than they?"
Matthew 6:25-26

HE HELPED ME BY the shoulder and with a low but firm voice he said, *"Emely, you have to remember that you are still a professor in the University. You still work FOR the University. You should never be identified with any group of students."*

That was the second time that I was told exactly the same words. The first time I heard this was from another university official, but it sounded more of a concern. But this time, what I heard sounded more of a warning.

That night I could not sleep. The image of him and what came from his mouth were unlikely to be uttered by a man of position, I thought. That very night, I made my decision. I am leaving.

I was a *"mother hen"* to fifty-one Filipino scholars in this university here in Korea. Though unofficially and without any formal appointment, nor even part of my teaching duties or hours, I took it upon myself to take care of them. We were like one big family. They were all my children.

One of the students was apparently involved in a sensitive issue. Despite negotiations and request for due process, the student was asked to leave the dormitory the soonest possible time, at the height of the cold winter.

I personally went to the dormitory administrator and begged him, *"Please, let me take care of him. I don't mind having him live temporarily with me, my son, and my daughter. Just don't make him leave now (that time he was supposed to leave before 5PM). It's so cold outside and he does not have a family here. He has nowhere to go."* I cannot control my tears anymore.

"But Professor, your house is still part of the university." I cried. *"You see, are we not supposed to be the first ones to live what the Bible says? Offer your home to a homeless? It's very simple, right?"* I explained. *"But…Professor,"* he continued, *"I perfectly understand you, and I agree with you. But this is the decision of the higher authorities."* I calmed down but still I was crying inside. I was helpless. We had no choice but to let him leave in the midst of that cold, gloomy afternoon. But Thank God, a good samaritan, a Filipino worker, offered him a home. He was still able to finish his Master's Degree with flying colors.

I made my decision, I am resigning. I wrote my resignation letter and submitted it to the office. A few days later, I got some calls from those who learned about my resignation. Two of them were sorry but they supported my decision. In fact. they said I gave them some kind of strength to make a stand against the issue. I heard a few months later that these two also left their positions. I was affirmed.

A week after I filed my resignation, I got a phone call from the Finance office. *"Hello Professor. This is from the Finance Office. We will not pay you anymore for January and February. You still need to pay additional cash bla bla bla…"* I could not understand her anymore. I felt like heaven and earth fell on me. I was dumbfounded and my throat was dry. After gathering my senses I answered, *"Sorry, can I just visit your office now? I don't understand what you are saying."*

I hurriedly went to their office, and though the explanation was clear (the policy was never explained to me in the beginning), my mind just refused to accept their reason. All through the three terms I had with the university, I asked them to give me enough classes and comply with what was stipulated in the contract regarding the number of hours I had to teach. Yet, I always got the same answer, *"Don't worry."* But now that I was leaving they wouldn't release my two months salary because I haven't taught enough hours. How could this be? My daughter and son were with me. How could we survive in a foreign land with me not having pay for the next two months?

That same night, I received an email from the Philippine Embassy through the PhilRPG (Philippine Resource Persons Group) yahoo group. A certain university was in need of foreign professors. I immediately updated my Curriculum Vitae and sent it to the email indicated in the information. When I woke up the next day, I received an acknowledgement email and I was requested for an interview on that same day. I met a lady in Seoul, a friend of the administrator, from the recruiting university. After a short talk, she called up the administrator and I was requested to travel down South to meet the official. That was already around 4 o'clock in the afternoon when my friend drove me to the Express Bus Terminal where I was off to meet the administrator.

While I was on my way, I can't help but wonder again how the power of God moved in my life. I was met by the official at the bus terminal. We went to his office for an interview and at that very instant, I was hired as he immediately wanted me to help in their recruitment and partnership programs with Philippine universities. Everything happened so fast. God knew exactly when to pick me up.

We were supposed to vacate the house in my previous university because my resignation will take effect in a few days. The problem was we had no place to go for the time being. I had my daughter and my son with me and I didn't have money. I was totally broke. I and my children were, so to speak, homeless. But friends came to the rescue.

The Lord is, indeed, generous and a great provider. We were *"adopted"* by benevolent and good people, Flor and Mareng Nenette, in their apartment. Bringing with us all our things, we moved to their place. A few weeks later, with the help of Jojo and Flor, we transferred to our new place in Gyeongju.

The room provided by the university became my home for three semesters. After more than a year, I had to move again to a new house. This was my tenth accommodation in my eight years in Korea and I prayed, *"Lord, let this be my last house in Korea. Please let me stay longer in my new house,"* without having any idea what kind of house my new university will give me.

In my Korea sojourn, I have moved from house to house as the need arose. Initially, I lived in a small room/boarding house for about a week. Then to save money, I did a homestay with one Korean family for a few months. After, I moved to the

Philippine Center. I also rented a small room at the rooftop of a villa which is super hot in summer and super cold in winter. When I got sick, one of my friends offered me to stay with her. I thought that maybe this is really the life of a migrant, an NPA (No Permanent Address). So, I perfectly understood the feelings of that student who was sent out of the dormitory because I, myself, have been through it.

When I was a missionary for the Philippine Center, I had no permanent job. I had to make both ends meet to be able to support my four growing children. I had to do freelance tutoring to nuns, priests, seminarians, and some office workers. When I received a phone call or a text message that said, *"Sorry Emely our class today is cancelled."* I felt so bad because it meant a reduction in my children's pocket money to school or tuition fee.

My life in Korea is not far from that of a household or factory worker. Actually, some of them are even financially better than I. With all humility, I am not embarrassed to admit that I've borrowed money here and there, begged for advance remittances, requested for loans and others just to make both ends meet. As a single parent, my chidren depended solely on me and I, too, had to sustain myself in a foreign land. But thank God He has provided me with people like--Flor, Matet, Precy, Lea, Norma, Ellen, Lyn, Bunso, Anj, Carol, Elena, Alan, Juvie, Digoy, Rica, Ivy, Nomar, Tita Fe, Hermie and Kate, Joeffrey, Jhoanna, Ardelle, Cynthia, Mommy Ineng (Elisea), Joy, Fr. Alvin, Sr. Angel, Fr. Augustine, and all others that I may have forgotten--who have helped me survive, financially, morally, and spiritually. They may not have realized it, but they have saved lives. They were all God sent, angels here on earth. They were answers to my prayers. I will be eternally grateful to each and everyone and I pray that God reward them dearly for their kindness and generosity.

When I moved to my tenth house (my current housing), I cried in awe and gratitude for the house that He gave me. He gave me a house too big for myself, so cozy, and very accessible to my new school. When I opened the door, the white wall and ceiling was like heaven to me. *"Dear God, I promise that this house will not be mine alone, but it will be open to anyone who needs a place to stay, a bed to sleep, and a venue for counseling, prayer, and even meditation."* In my three years of stay here, it has served its purpose. It has become a halfway house for anyone who needs a place to stay.   I believe this is such a great blessing meant to be shared to others.

This is my way of returning the glory back to God, and for all the favors and love I have received from countless people in my life. I may not be able to return all the goodness back to these people personally, but I am returning them to other people who are in need, not only financially or materially, but also emotionally or spiritually.

That's how God provides. He provides through people and let the ripple effect of love continue. This is the miracle--the miracle of the heart.

Worry not! What kept me going was God's promise, *"Look at the birds of the air; they do not sow or reap or store away in barns, and yet your heavenly Father feeds them."* In my eleven years in Korea, God has fulfilled this promise more than a hundred times in my life.

Friends do come to help every time I need them. I am always reminded that in the eyes of God, I am more important than the birds in the sky, that I am indeed loved by God, through people, through family, and through friends.

LET US PRAY...

Jesus, the greatest provider, you have always sustained me and my family's needs. You know exactly when to rescue us from our material, financial, and physiological needs. Thank you for the good health, for the good job, and for the very generous family and friends whose arms are always ready to help during our crisis. I pray that you bless each of them and their families. You Oh, Lord be the one to return the favors they have extended me. This I pray. AMEN.

POINTS TO PONDER...

1. Have you ever experienced financial/material crisis? To whom did you turn to for help?
2. Did you feel God providing for your needs during these times? In what way?

3. Have you had a chance to say thank you to those who helped you? Have you helped others also in your own little way?

TALK TO GOD...

____
____
____
____
____
____

19 GOD KNOWS BEST

Trust in the Lord and do good;
Dwell in the land and cultivate faithfulness.
Delight yourself in the Lord;
And He will give you the desires of your heart.
Psalm 37:3-4

"EXCUSE ME," I heard one lady while she pulled a chair and sat beside me. *"Yes. What can I do for you?" "Can you help me, please? Our university is hiring foreign teachers and I need one foreign faculty for my department. Can you help me find one?"* **Without hesitation, I said,** *"Sure! Why not? That's what I do for in my university now. I help in the recruitment of Filipino professors."*

This happened during the Seollal (Chinese New Year) in 2012. I was facilitating a spiritual retreat together with Fr. Chris de Guzman to the El Shaddai Prayer Partners Community Daegu Chapter. We were finishing our dinner when this lady suddenly appeared out of nowhere.

Later, she introduced herself as the Social Welfare Department Head of Catholic University of Daegu. Coming from the same discipline as I am, we spoke of the same things and have become comfortable with each other, so I said, *"I can help you, don't worry. But I don't have anybody in mind at the moment. I will update you later."* Then she took a piece of paper and wrote my name and phone number. She wrote hers and gave it to me. When she learned that I was teaching in another university, she offered, *"Why don't you apply?"* With this words, my face brightened and my heart leaped with excitement. But I honestly answered, *"I'm sorry. I can't because I still have a contract with my current university."* But, I assured her I will look for someone for her department.

When we parted at the dining hall of the retreat house that night, I felt like Angel Gabriel came to greet me from above. She joined us in our last Eucharistic Celebration and I promised her I will keep her posted. Her sweet smile and warmth left me with amazement.

After the holidays, I met my superior in my university. With enthusiasm, I told him the whole story and I even mentioned that I was offered to apply. I didn't mind him knowing after all. Immediately after my story he said, *"Emely, your God is a wonderful God!"* I was deeply touched. A remark like this from a Buddhist is really amazing. Again, I felt an angel whispered to me, *"Emely, your God is a wonderful God."*

"Then, apply! Go! I understand your situation, Emely. And I know you will have more opportunities to grow professionally if you move there because you will be teaching a subject that is close to your heart and you will be able to do research," This was another unexpected reaction from him. *"Are you serious?* I asked. *"I am serious! Of course, we need you here and you've been helping us a lot. But your future is more important. I understand."* I had his blessing.

With all honesty, I was at that point of my career when I wanted to move to another place, another country, another surrounding. I was not sure, but I wanted a different environment where I could do something else. I tried sending applications to Singapore, Middle East, Thailand, and other Korean universities but nobody gave an affirmative answer, except for one Korean university who tested my Korean language ability. As expected, I failed.

April was about to end. The recruitment time in Korean universities was almost over. The idea of applying to CUD came to mind. I checked their website and found out the deadline of application was over. But just the same, I sent my application on April 28th. In my mind, if it's God's will, He will make it happen. I did not hear anything from them so I did not bother to follow up anymore.

On June 4, 2012, I received an email from the Department Head sending me the good news that out of eight applicants, I was the one considered. There was no interview at all. I was instructed to submit additional requirements the soonest time possible.

I immediately informed my superior about the new offer that has come. I felt he was happy for me, too. He congratulated me and he informed the University President on my anticipated resignation. I was told that the President wanted to keep me in the university. In fact, I was being offered a raise but I told my superiors I wouldn't also be happy receiving that much while my colleagues will not be receiving the same amount. I said I have already made my decision and was ready to start a career in another workplace. I finally submitted my resignation letter.

Two weeks before I left, I wrote a thank you letter to the President. I expressed my sincerest gratitude for giving me this opportunity to be part of the university and do some administration-related jobs as part of my service to the institution. Without elaborating further, I also articulated the big help the university has extended me after that unfortunate experience I had from the other university.

Before I left, I visited the President personally in her office together with my two superiors. *"Thank you so much for the opportunity you've given me to work with you and the university. I really appreciate your generous offer. I'd really love to stay longer but I've made my final decision."* Her answer was unbelievable. She said, *"Emely, thank you. And I'm sorry if I did not show my appreciation to your efforts much earlier."* I just smiled. She added, *"The door of the university is always open for you."* What a graceful exit!

When I met my new Department Head to submit my requirements, she said, *"Professor, everything is from God. Everything is providential."* With all affirmation I answered back, *"Indeed, Professor. God made it happen. That time we met at the retreat house, that was a perfect time made by God for you and me to meet."* She hugged me tightly and whispered, *"Let's pray for one another."* I felt an angel hug me tightly and welcome me to the heavens.

My heart is full of desires--countless desires. Many times I don't even have to mention them in prayer but God knows exactly what is in my heart. I trust that in His most perfect time He will grant them, that one day He will just surprise me, just as what happened in this story.

God planted me in this new place so that I can bloom according to the ways of the Lord. I am beset with new challenges, with new roles, and with a new mission to fulfill.

Trust in the Lord, be faithful to Him, and He will grant the desires of your heart, in His perfect time because He definitely knows best!

LET US PRAY...

You are indeed a God of surprises, Lord. You know the desires of my heart that even before I tell them to you, you have answered them already. You know what is best for me and my family and so I continue offering them to you. Lead us, dear Lord, where we can bloom and spread your love more and more. I ask this in your Holy name. AMEN.

POINTS TO PONDER...

1. What unexpected blessings have you received from God?
2. How did you show God your appreciation for these unexpected blessings from God?
3. Have you ever shared these blessings to others?

TALK TO GOD...

____

____

____

____

____

____

20 YOU'LL WEEP NO MORE

Yet the LORD longs to be gracious to you;
he rises to show you compassion.
For the LORD is a God of justice.
Blessed are all who wait for him!
O people of Zion, who live in Jerusalem,
you will weep no more.
How gracious he will be when you cry for help!
As soon as he hears, he will answer you.
Isaiah 30:18-19

GOOD EVENING! ANA? KAMUSTA KA? *Madi ka maexciten? Adda naawat ko decisionen kabsat," (How are you? Aren't you excited anymore? I already received the decision, sister)* **a text message I got from my eldest sister, Merilyn. I shouted in excitement. My two friends who were with me were surprised. I grabbed my phone and immediately called my sister. She said,** *"you can start using your maiden* *name."* **Honestly, when I heard this I could not exactly** *"name"* **how I felt. I could not get hold of the proper word to describe my feelings.**

Upon arriving in my apartment, I prayed. I offered a special prayer to God for thanksgiving. I was grateful that after many years, after all the twists and turns of events, it was finally granted. I know my family and friends were all happy for me. I chatted with Renz and her question struck me. *"Pero Ma, are you happy?"* **(But Ma, are you happy?)** *"Hmmm… kinakapa ko pa. Mixed eh."***(Hmmm.. I'm still trying to get hold of it. I have mixed feelings).** I answered. I kept quiet for a while, took a deep sigh, closed my eyes, and when I opened them I discovered how I felt. **JUSTICE!** Yes, I know God plans marriage to be a union that is inseparable between a husband and a wife. I knew that in my heart. But God knows better. God knows what I deserve. *"Salamat sa Diyos!"* **(Thank God!)**

I know it was just a piece of paper with the judge's signature but the dissolution of my marriage meant a lot to me. After everything that I have been through, I have finally regained my self-worth. The dignity that I have, somehow, lost is back. That as I stride the path towards my new life, I am leaving all the resentments and pains behind.

My nieces said, *"It came when we least expected it."* That's how God surprises us. He pours his blessings when we are resigned, when we have done all possible human interventions, and we cannot do anything but bend our knees in prayer and say, *"Lord, Thy will be done."*

Around September 2014, my sister got news that the case was dismissed because there was a *"little problem."* My sister insisted that I call my lawyer, which I did. He explained what the *"problem"* was but I was very firm on my stand. *"Attorney,"* I said, *"I will accept whatever the decision of the court will be. Favorable or unfavorable is okay with me. If the judge doesn't find merit in my case, then so be it."* Again, *"Lord, Thy will be done."*

After a week, my lawyer sent a text message to inform me that the court decision is out and the result is favorable. I got the shock of my life. What possibly could have happened that the decision was suddenly reversed? This remains to be a mystery to me, until today. But there's one thing I am very sure of--it was GOD who made a way! Definitely, this is His will and this is His way of showing justice to those who patiently wait for His compassion. I hold on to His promise --*"you will weep no more."*

June of 2008, after five years of separation, I consulted a lawyer who happens to be a family friend. I told him the whole story and he requested me to write my testimony which I did. It was not difficult for me to recall the past events because from the time I discovered that Rod cheated on me, I started to write in my journal. It was my way of coping with all the emotional and psychological turmoil he caused me. All the dates, time, place, and even text messages were all recorded in my journal.

Writing and recalling the events was painful and tearful, but therapeutic. I was able to write a twenty page testimony.

I submitted all the documents, took my psychological test, and finally on July 2, 2008, I signed an affidavit giving my lawyer authority to secure and verify other information and documents needed for the process. I started counting from that day on. However, I really don't know what happened, but the case was only filed in court two years after, exactly on July 2, 2010.

My appearance in court was traumatic and embarrassing, at the same time healing and therapeutic. Traumatic and embarrassing because I had to narrate everything, even the minutest details and use the exact demeaning words uttered by my husband. *"For documentation purposes, can you please tell this Honorable Court, the exact words that the respondent uttered?"* My lawyer summoned. I felt my stomach grumble, my hands clammy, and my body tremble. I had to muster all my energy and courage to be able to speak in front of the judge, the fiscal, my lawyer, two other lawyers and other people who were also scheduled for a court hearing that day in the same courtroom.

"With your permission and with due respect to Your Honorable Court, Your Honor, please allow me to say the exact words…" And yes!!! Uttering the same demeaning words, coming from my very own mouth, said with rage and agony, the deep buried pain, the pent up emotions that have been ignored for years were finally expressed. That was therapeutic and healing.

I did not mind at all who were listening, how many of them, and what their reactions were. All I cared about at that very moment was to be free and defend myself. All I wanted was to be heard. All I needed was for people to believe my testimony. Then I remembered a friend who went through annulment and told me, *"The whole process is not easy. You really have to brace yourself because you will have to recall the past. Recalling the past is horrible. You will have to go through an embarrassing moment."* I did. I went through a very humiliating, embarrassing, and humbling process. But what is done has been done. What else have I to hide? Much as I wanted to protect our marriage, to keep it confidential and make it private, ultimately it was publicized.

One of my sisters, Ate Weng, who witnessed my torments, was also asked to testify in court. Thanks to the support of my family. They remained to be my strenghth all the way. My brother, Kuya Tante, and niece, Atty. Sen, had to go home to Ilocos to attend the hearing only to find out that the schedule was cancelled, the judge was on leave, and some other reasons might have perhaps caused the delay.

When I and my children decided to see my husband after ten years of separation on March 2014, I promised God that never again will I insist on the annulment. I did not follow it up anymore. *"Lord, your will be done,"* was my prayer.

September 30, 2014 the court decided in favor of our marriage annulment. He died on November 17, 2014 without him knowing that we have become un-married. I was not interested anymore on the Decree of Finality from the Solicitor General's Office. However, because of this woman who was introduced to me by my mother-in-law and who was asking me to pay Rod's debt of 2,000 USD, my niece, Atty. Sen, advised me to check at the SolGen's office. The decree of finality will spare me from further obligations. True enough, the Decree of Finality was approved by the SolGen's Office on October 22, 2014, less than a month before Rod passed away. In the eyes of the law, our marriage was already dissolved even before he passed away. But in the eyes of God, we remained husband and wife until his very last breath.

A very extraordinary story!

The wait was long, but it was worth the wait. I was made to realize a lot of things in the process of waiting. I learned to wait patiently, that patience is indeed a virtue, and to those who wait patiently, God rewards them with compassion. For the Lord is a God of justice. Blessed are all who wait for him for they will weep no more.

LET US PRAY...

Dear God of Justice, thank you for redeeming me from my humiliation, from making public what was supposed to be private and sacred. Thank you for giving me enough courage to compose myself and face the many people hear my story. I know you were just there beside me and I know it was you who willed this to happen. Now that you gave me the justice

I deserve, may you use me as your instrument as I journey with other women who may be facing the same crisis that I went through. AMEN.

POINTS TO PONDER...

1. Was there any chance when you had to share your deepest struggles with the person you love, to a friend or a family member? How did you feel?
2. Are there times when you feel like giving up on your marriage/relationship? What is keeping you until now in that relationship?
3. How sacred is marriage for you? What probable reason(s) can you give for a marriage to be dissolved?

TALK TO GOD...

____

____

____

____

____

____

ABOUT THE AUTHOR

Prof. Emely Dulig Dicolen, PhD is a Professor at the Social Welfare Department of Catholic University of Daegu (CUD), South Korea. She is the President of the Association of Filipino Educators in Korea (AFEK), and an adviser to Filipino organizations in Korea, namely, Pinoy Iskolars sa Korea (PIKO) and the Filipino EPS Workers Association (FEWA). She was appointed as Coordinator for the ASIA Region of the Diaspora to Development Network, and is recently elected as a Founding Board Member of an international NGO, the Global Saemaul Development Network (GSDN) based in South Korea.

The author is a recipient of several awards including The

2010 Outstanding Filipino Overseas under the Banaag Category by the Office of the President of the Philippines; The 2013 Centennial Awardee under the Education Category by the College of the Holy Spirit Manila; and The 2008 Outstanding Filipino in South Korea; Gawad Giovanni Jaron by the Filipino EPS Workers Association.

She has authored and co-authored books, articles, and publications. In 2010, she wrote "And GOD Smiled Back", published by St. Paul's. She has co-authored textbooks, entitled "On the Way to God" and "The Beauty of Doing Good."

Emely is a product of a well-rounded Catholic Education: the University of Santo Tomas, Manila, Philippines for her Ph.D. in Development Education; the Ateneo de Manila University for her M.A. in Theological Studies; and the College of the Holy Spirit Manila for her BS in Education, Major in Religious Education. She was also a Research Fellow of the Korea Foundation for Advanced Studies (KFAS).

As an administrator and teacher, she was a concurrent Dean of the Graduate School and the Arts and Sciences Department of the Colegio de San Juan de Letran Calamba; Campus Minister and Director for Research and Extension of the First Asia Institute of Technology and Humanities (FAITH); Theology Chairperson of the College of the Holy Spirit Manila; and Education Chairperson of the Hyehwadong Filipino Catholic Community (HFCC). She also taught in the following universities: Laguna College of Business and Arts (LCBA), Catholic University of Korea (CUK), Gyeongju University (GU), Hankuk University of Foreign Studies (HUFS), and the Korean Missionary Society (KMS).

For more information about the author, you may email her at emelyabagat@gmail.com or read her blog http://maestrosendong.wordpress.com/ for more inspirational reflections and insights.

www.ingramcontent.com/pod-product-compliance
Lightning Source LLC
LaVergne TN
LVHW020746200726
843506LV00009B/901